D0279477

CultureShock!
A Survival Guide to Customs and Etiquette

Switzerland

Max Oettli

Marshall Cavendish
Editions

This second edition published in 2012 by:
Marshall Cavendish Corporation
99 White Plains Road
Tarrytown, NY 10591-9001
www.marshallcavendish.us

First published in 2009

Copyright © Marshall Cavendish International (Asia) Private Limited
All rights reserved

No part of this publication may be reproduced, stored in a retrieval system
or transmitted, in any form or by any means, electronic, mechanical,
photocopying, recording or otherwise, without the prior permission of
the copyright owner. Request for permission should be addressed to the
Publisher, Marshall Cavendish International (Asia) Private Limited, 1 New
Industrial Road, Singapore 536196. Tel: (65) 6213 9300, fax: (65) 6285 4871.
E-mail: genref@sg.marshallcavendish.com

The publisher makes no representation or warranties with respect to the
contents of this book, and specifically disclaims any implied warranties or
merchantability or fitness for any particular purpose, and shall in no event be
liable for any loss of profit or any other commercial damage, including but not
limited to special, incidental, consequential, or other damages.

Other Marshall Cavendish Offices:
Marshall Cavendish International (Asia) Private Limited. 1 New Industrial
Road, Singapore 536196 ■ Marshall Cavendish International. PO Box 65829,
London EC1P 1NY, UK ■ Marshall Cavendish International (Thailand) Co Ltd.
253 Asoke, 12th Flr, Sukhumvit 21 Road, Klongtoey Nua, Wattana, Bangkok
10110, Thailand ■ Marshall Cavendish (Malaysia) Sdn Bhd, Times Subang,
Lot 46, Subang Hi-Tech Industrial Park, Batu Tiga, 40000 Shah Alam, Selangor
Darul Ehsan, Malaysia

Marshall Cavendish is a trademark of Times Publishing Limited

ISBN: 978-0-7614-0050-9

Please contact the publisher for the Library of Congress catalog number

Printed in Singapore by Times Printers Pte Ltd

Photo Credits:
All black and white photos by the author except pages 15 and 26–27
(Photolibrary). All colour photos from Photolibrary. ■ Cover: Sculpture of
giant fork in Lake Geneva at Vevey (Photolibrary)

All illustrations by TRIGG

ABOUT THE SERIES

Culture shock is a state of disorientation that can come over anyone who has been thrust into unknown surroundings, away from one's comfort zone. *CultureShock!* is a series of trusted and reputed guides which has, for decades, been helping expatriates and long-term visitors to cushion the impact of culture shock whenever they move to a new country.

Written by people who have lived in the country and experienced culture shock themselves, the books provide all the information necessary for anyone to cope with these feelings of disorientation more effectively. The guides are written in a style that is easy to read and cover a range of topics that will arm readers with enough advice, hints and tips to make their lives as normal as possible again.

Each book is structured in the same manner. It begins with the first impressions that visitors will have of that city or country. To understand a culture, one must first understand the people—where they came from, who they are, the values and traditions they live by, as well as their customs and etiquette. This is covered in the first half of the book.

Then on with the practical aspects—how to settle in with the greatest of ease. Authors walk readers through topics such as how to find accommodation, get the utilities and telecommunications up and running, enrol the children in school and keep in the pink of health. But that's not all. Once the essentials are out of the way, venture out and try the food, enjoy more of the culture and travel to other areas. Then be immersed in the language of the country before discovering more about the business side of things.

To round off, snippets of basic information are offered before readers are 'tested' on the customs and etiquette of the country. Useful words and phrases, a comprehensive resource guide and list of books for further research are also included for easy reference.

CONTENTS

Dedication vi

Acknowledgements vii

Map of Switzerland viii

Chapter 1
First Impressions 1

Welcome, and Don't Forget
to Shut the Door Behind You   2

Personal Experiences   7

Small is Beautiful   9

Chapter 2
A Tour of Switzerland 12

The Shape of the Land   13

The Myth of Cleanliness   19

History in 5 Easy Sections   25

A Peasant Confederacy   43

Chapter 3
The Swiss People 55

National Characteristics   56

Townies and Rurals   60

Chapter 4
Swiss Society 67

Perceptions   68

Playing Soldiers   76

Virtue and Vice   82

Trouble in Toyland   90

A Comedy of Manners   94

Chapter 5
Welcome On Board 99

Papering It Over   100

Fixed Abodes   104

Banking   113

I'm the Taxman   114

In Sickness and in Health   116

Schooldays   118

Transport   121

Shopping   132

Chapter 6
Food and Entertaining 138

How the Swiss Feed   139

Shopping for Food   141

Swiss Specialities   145

What do the Swiss Drink?   159

Eating Out   162

Dinner Invitations   162

Chapter 7
Enjoying Switzerland 166

Getting Some Air   167

Art and Culture   178

Swiss Feasts   182

Chapter 8

The Swiss Languages   193

Swiss-German	196
Swiss-French	198
Learning the Languages	199

Chapter 9

Working Life   202

Wages	203
Hours of Work	205
Appearance	207
Generally Speaking	207

Chapter 10

Switzerland at a Glance   209

Famous Swiss	213
Acronyms in Switzerland	224
Places of Interest	225

Culture Quiz	229
Do's and Don'ts	234
Glossary	237
Resource Guide	240
Further Reading	243
About the Author	245
Index	246

DEDICATION

I lovingly dedicate this book to my wife Simone, and our sons Jean René and Lucas.

Thank you to the helpful editors at Marshall Cavendish who made this project worthwhile. Thank you also to various people in Switzerland for giving me valuable feedback.

MAP OF SWITZERLAND

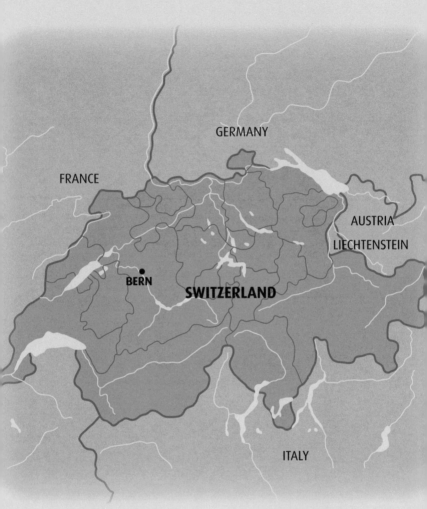

FIRST IMPRESSIONS

CHAPTER 1

"Switzerland doesn't exist."
—Slogan for Swiss presence at the
1992 World Expo in Seville

Leabharlanna Poiblí Chathair Bhaile Átha Cliath
Dublin City Public Libraries

WELCOME, AND DON'T FORGET TO SHUT THE DOOR BEHIND YOU

You'll enjoy Switzerland. It is a pocket-size country with a rich and varied landscape, four national languages, and an impressive mixture of different cultural and ethnic groups. This is largely related to its unique position at the rather rocky nexus of a historically quarrelsome continent.

If you like water, Switzerland has some of Europe's longest rivers springing from its mountains, and numerous lakes, from chilly, clear, high-altitude puddles to the biggest one in western Europe. If you like mountains, it has more peaks than any other country in Europe, and thousands of climbing, walking and skiing routes.

If you like conviviality, there are cafés, concert halls and other places to hang out catering to all imaginable tastes. If culture is your thing, Switzerland boasts some of Europe's finest museums; most cities have many theatres and concert halls, and there are half a dozen fine orchestras, and countless jazz and pop musicians to listen to. If you like food and wine, the variety is rich and full of pleasant surprises.

If you're picking up this book, you have probably decided to come to Switzerland: you want to come here to study, you have a job lined up, or your partner has, and you want a little help to find your way around. Well, you're in luck. Switzerland is a pretty straightforward place, and once you've grasped the codes that govern daily life (similar in many respects to

The Matterhorn, one of the world's best-known mountains, rises at the border with Italy.

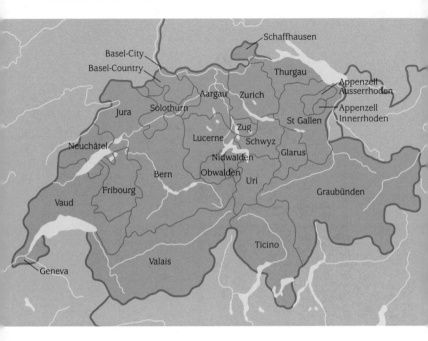

those in most European countries), you'll quickly find which levers to pull to get the goodies you want.

What you must bear in mind, though, is that Switzerland is a country where people tend to identify closely with the cantons they live in—and that *you'll* be living in—and that from canton to canton, there are differences not just in language, but also in the more subtle values that people live by, and expect you to conform to.

The Swiss are on the whole a rather discreet and private crowd, and transgressions, such as your baby throwing a tantrum in a quiet restaurant, can have some rather unexpected consequences. In Italy, say, you'd be likely to have the little brat passed around a few mammas and returned to you calmed; here you're more likely to get icy stares from the blue-rinse brigade.

The other thing you must be very careful of here is to have your own life in order, in terms of having your papers sorted out, your home address on the municipal register, and all that very slightly Kafkaesque stuff. You are in a small and rather well-policed country here, and you cannot hide behind another identity as you might in a mega-city like London, Rome or Rio.

But assuming you are more or less sorted, you'll have a lot of freedom and latitude and the country is yours to enjoy and live in—whether you've just stepped off a train from Bucharest or Beijing, or you trace your ancestors back to old William Tell himself.

Here You Are

You'll probably find it quite easy to find your way around when you arrive here. Our biggest cities are a few huts compared to Los Angeles, Kuala Lumpur or Hong Kong, and you'll be able to find the landmarks, main roads, rivers and lakes that sort out your directions within a day or two. Your bank card will probably work at the countless corner cashpoints. You'll find prices clearly marked on anything you may want to buy. Lost? Ask your way. It happens to me all the time, and most people here are proud of their linguistic skills. You will almost certainly find someone who speaks English, Spanish, Portuguese, Turkish or some of the Eastern European languages quite quickly.

It is best to find some form of accommodation before you arrive. You should not count on locals to put you up at their homes, unless that has been arranged previously, as most people here live in rather small flats. Locals may, however, be able to help you find accommodation for the first few weeks. My wife and I put up for three very pleasant weeks in a university residence while waiting for our Geneva flat to become free.

You will quickly pick up lots more advice if you are in a work or study environment—about the nuts and bolts of the place, how to get around, how to sort out the initial formalities and all that. Making friends is a rather slower process, but it will come, it will come.

Where Are You From?

Manoeuvring in Switzerland depends a great deal on where you come from. It would be straightforward for a German, a Belgian, an Austrian or a Frenchman to find his way around rapidly; he would find a more or less familiar language and a broadly similar structure of life and customs around him. So too would Italians moving to the Swiss-Italian region. But if you're from Tartary, Texas, Tanzania or Thailand, you might take a little more time to get to know the ways of the place and to feel comfortable.

Call it culture shock—getting used to the customs and ways of a new place. Much lies in the details, the small things that make life turn around, in avoiding the rough edges, and navigating as smoothly as possible through the initial adaptation.

That is what this book will try to do.

Max's Story

As my wife and I arrived here a few decades ago from New Zealand, it might be worth telling our story and drawing some general principles from it.

Having both been born in Europe, we had arguably a bit of a headstart on others. Still, it took us a while to acclimatise ourselves to the discreet charm of the place, finding the northern region where we had settled rather coldly polite, the people poised in limbo between inquisitiveness and indifference. I worked in a factory initially and quickly became pals with Charlie the Turk and Pacifico the Italian. The fact that I was Swiss put a slight barrier between us though; as a native I was supposed to have a certain attitude towards the foreign labourers which they for their part seemed as willing to enforce as some of my countrymen.

Later, my wife and I worked for a tree farm, staking apple tree saplings as the bumptious, unpleasant boss watched from his private swimming pool to see how we were progressing on our backbreaking trek. We acquired a little car, and were soon merrily chugging around in search of the lovely places that surrounded our valley: fairytale forests, picturesque little towns and the occasional whiff of Zürich, where we rushed back into a kind of Swiss-accented English-language scene, with bookshops, cinemas and café terraces.

Geneva, where we moved after a few months, suited us better. We knew by now that Switzerland was an incredible patchwork, and we found that Geneva had a historical and cultural identity that was not overly Swiss, with people of all colours and shapes in its streets. We were comfortable in the French language and cultural environment; proud that Geneva takes more progressive positions in federal policy votes (though often in vain); and delighted to be located at one of Europe's nodes, with direct lines to the Alps, to Italy and to the north.

PERSONAL EXPERIENCES

We talked to friends and listened to them when they first arrived. Here are some of their stories.

Henry is a tall American colleague of my wife's. He likes Switzerland well enough, but finds all of the dimensions of the place minute. He also can't understand why Geneva and Lausanne, 60 km (37.3 miles) apart, bother being different cities. He points and laughs when a Smart Mini-car comes buzzing up; cringes when his king-size bed almost completely fills the bedroom of his Geneva apartment; and stares in disbelief at the tiny expensive servings on his restaurant plate.

Another friend, from Iran, remarks on the incredible variety of the population. He tells us that in Teheran, heads turn if someone of African or Asian descent walks by. He also remarks on the number of ladies who seem to walk 'free' here, bright-eyed and busy and clad in all colours.

A Senegalese student, whose wife has stayed behind with the children, tells me how lonely and homesick he is, but a few months later he's found others from Senegal to eat with, watch videos with, and visit the mosque with.

South Americans also tend to group with people of the same origins; the Chilean 'singsong' parties are famous in the region, as are the Afro-Maghrebian restaurants where the music comes as spicy as the sauces.

For my wife and I, partly because of our being born in Switzerland, we have gone pretty native as time goes on. We have more friends who speak French (or Spanish, German, etc) than who speak English, and seem to know very few local residents of Kiwi origin. Many of the Swiss we know take pride in their origin, so an American friend's husband is Swiss-German from the Argovie region, another friend comes from the Valais region, and good neighbour, Nico, is Swiss-Italian right down to his taste in wine and coffee.

I can see in our sons—who are benefiting from a Swiss education—acceptance of certain Swiss values in their day-to-day lives. Our elder son has a good and highly pragmatic notion of what makes Switzerland work; he set up the Internet site for the organisation that helps young Swiss avoid military conscription by doing civilian national service. The younger one has an incredible array of friends from all imaginable corners of the earth, and has the Swiss passion for travel in his blood.

What this book will do is show you a few of the ropes that make this particular ship sail—to get you comfortable here, both with the land and its people. Never forget, everyone comes from somewhere; populations have always been on the move, be it in search of new worlds and fortunes—as in the migrations in Polynesia or in the rush to the American West—or in flight from tragedy, such as the East Europeans or the Irish escaping from starvation, echoed now by the boat people of Asia and Africa, who wash up half-dead on suspicious and intolerant shores.

Switzerland was built on immigration long before it was thought of as a nation state. The Goths, the Romans, the Burgundians and the French Huguenots all came here on their weary way and found ways to live. Later the Italians of the Piedmont taught us how to build; and in my lifetime there have been at least four waves of immigration, each bringing new values, a few problems, and a far richer place in their wake.

SMALL IS BEAUTIFUL

Switzerland is a small country. When the government received its latest generation of jetfighters some years ago, there was a certain amount of embarrassment all round. These 'Mach 2' machines were designed as interceptors, but were quite simply unusable over Switzerland: they would have shot far into one of the neighbouring countries by the time they had half finished a manoeuvre at that speed. Swiss air-force pilots go to southern Italy to do their training over the Mediterranean—entailing some rather complicated bilateral arrangements for a supposedly neutral country.

This smallness is certainly one of the first things a visitor to Switzerland is aware of. The place is smaller and less populous than many of the US states, and the initial amazement of most visitors is how such variety can be packed into so small a place. Much of the wide-open space of Switzerland and also

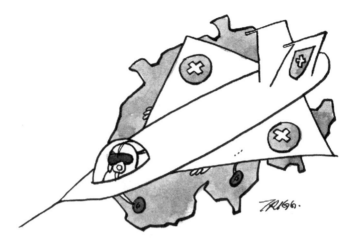

its beauty is in the Alps, for Switzerland is the junction of the European alpine massive, with the liveable spaces tucked into the valleys and on the shores of the many lovely lakes and rivers there. From the mountains you will often have a view of three countries.

Not only linguistically but in other ways too, the smallness of Switzerland in no way means uniformity. Sure, the trains whisper around on time at all levels, the mailboxes are all yellow and the car number plates all have a little Swiss shield on them along with the flag of the Canton.

On the other hand, in every canton the policemen have different uniforms. Fribourg farms are different from Bern farms—just 10 km (6.2 miles) down the road. The lush green along the shores of the Doubs in the Jura is another nuance from the rocky streams in the Grisons at the other end of the country. Eastern Swiss-German towns with their half-timbered houses and cobblestone streets are a world away from the Italianate alleys that wind around the towns of Ticino with their verticals and yellow distempered walls. Up north it's fresh and breezy, the air is clear, the colours bright. In the south, the wine is sweeter and lemons grow against stone walls.

Being small means that networks form quite easily and quickly among people of the country, although there is always the question of language. The contacts I have in Bern and Zürich—cultural, political, professional and casual—generally e-mail or telephone in French, but if we meet, with others present, German is used. The law requires all government publications to be in the three main national languages, and the Swiss go to considerable efforts to make this a reality. As for documents that may be important for other ethnic groups, these are often translated into the relevant languages.

Swiss Army Knife

Compact, efficient and multipurpose.

I open my Swiss army knife and joyfully attack almost any of the endless objects that clutter up my life: adjust the brakes on my son's bicycle, peel a grape for my beloved, repair a power plug, pick a lock if I'm into burgling, open a bottle of local wine (officer's knife only—the soldiers' version has a beer bottle opener—*noblesse oblige*)—the countless actions that a man's life is made up of. It gets quickly to the point where I feel unhappy if my knife gets mislaid, in a cranny behind the couch, in the car door, wherever... Sure, it's no big deal when the standard model is the price of a cafeteria lunch, but you'll have lost something which you've lovingly kept clean and sharpened on the oilstone in the kitchen and is part of your essential Swissness.

So the Swiss Army knife is more than an institution or a way of life, it is also a symbol of the way Switzerland runs and is constituted. First, the gender thing. Switzerland's traditions are masculine (women have only been voting on national issues for some three decades) and the versatile little feller is definitely designed for the man's trouser pocket, along with the other bits of bloke's stuff in there.

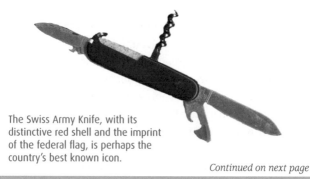

The Swiss Army Knife, with its distinctive red shell and the imprint of the federal flag, is perhaps the country's best known icon.

Continued on next page

Continued from previous page

Second, the look is definitely related to the Swiss nation: it is red; the Swiss Federal flag ornaments its smooth sides; the teeth are visible but discreet. It is efficient and elegant but of limited scope—I wouldn't try to take apart a fuel injection pump or a watch with it. So it is with Swiss democracy: vote by all means, but only on the understanding that the machine ticks on no matter what you do; far larger interests are at work. The gnomes of Zürich are all too real.

Thirdly, its multifunctionality could be related to the federal structure of the place. Switzerland is a small country, but a varied one. Each region has its language, its traditions and its history. The cantons each have their individual story to tell, their origin myths, their customs and their dialects. Yet, like the elaborate mechanism of the red handle with its white cross and steel claws, each element is attached to the other and the whole forms a unit—an indispensable pocket-sized tool, capable of harming, sure, but above all, of fixing and whittling things into shape.

You are here on a mission. As a student or an expatriate perhaps, or as a traveller who'd like to stay awhile, or as an immigrant ambitious to make your life and your family's here.

You will need far more than this little book in the long run, but I hope it will be of some use, to give you a few bits of advice and turn you towards other sources of practical help. Whatever happens, your experience here will be a positive one, and you will learn a lot, enjoy a lot, spiced with the occasional moment of exasperation during your stay in this beautiful little country.

A TOUR OF SWITZERLAND

CHAPTER 2

"Back to the hills!"
—Bob Dylan

THE SHAPE OF THE LAND

Switzerland is a small, landlocked country; at the same time, though, many of its borders are water. In the north-east the beautiful Bodensee (Lake Constance) creates a frontier with Germany in the north and Austria in the east. The Rhine, snaking out of the lake, divides north Switzerland from the Baden-Württemberg and Black Forest regions of Germany. In the south, western Europe's largest lake, Lake Geneva (Lac Léman), makes a border between Switzerland and the Savoy region of France. In the last few decades, a gargantuan engineering effort has been made to make the lakes clean and pleasant, and we can now swim in them when the weather is hot. Most of Switzerland's other frontiers with Italy, France and Austria are essentially the summits of mountains or the ridges of the giant Jura range which follows the French border from Basel to Geneva.

Ah the mountains! Switzerland may not boast Europe's highest peak (Mont Blanc is on the French side of the French-Italian border), but it has more peaks over 4,000 m (13,000 ft) than any other European country. Not surprisngly, skiing, snowboarding and other mountain sports are rather good here. But as a consequence only a third of its territory is habitable. A third of its territory? I peer with some perplexity into the *Times Atlas*. In a country that would fit ten times into the state of California, a third means something in the order of Northern Ireland, Gabon or Hawaii. A quick calculation—dividing Switzerland's population of 7.5 million over a third of its 41,300 sq km (15,946 sq miles)—and I end up with some impressive density figures. At some 471 souls per sq km, Switzerland's density is closer to Taiwan than that of the Netherlands.

As a result, the standard urban settlement pattern is apartment blocks. The density in turn lends itself to one of the most developed service and transport infrastructures in the world. If the place had developed like Los Angeles or Sydney, there would quite simply not be any space that was not built up or which could be used for roads.

Once we leave the northern plateau where most of the population lives, the country becomes rather wrinkled with a pattern of lakes and mountains that make it one of the most attractive places in the world. Much care is lavished on the quality of the landscape: the forests and pastures are well-tended, and apart from the occasional eyesore, the infrastructure, bridges, roads, railroads and buildings appear to have been carefully inserted into the landscape or at least well enough made to become visual elements in their own right. The spectacular motorway overbridge structure that floats high over Chillon Castle in Montreux mirrors the 19th-century railway line that snakes past its fortified walls at lake level—spanning some eight centuries with a remarkable expression of continuity.

Swiss Toy Set
In his classic, *The Great Railway Bazaar*, Paul Theroux describes Switzerland as resembling a life-sized train set—with picturesque mountains tunnels and bridges, stations with geraniums in the windows, and endless little trains busily chugging in concert with funiculars, mountain rack-and-pinion trains, and paddle steamers on the lakes.

The Swiss rail system is legendary, but more recently a pretty good network of motorways and national highways has been added to the picture. The former are paid by a

Chillon Castle, on the shore of Lake Geneva, dates back to the 12th century.

user tax: every car using them must have a receipt pasted on its windscreen for a 40-franc fee. For the Swiss this is relatively light, for tourists often a source of annoyance.

The combination of watery mountains and busy urbanised valleys gave Switzerland its means for entering the world of manufacturing—with a good range of light industry powered by the cheaply produced hydro-electricity. Switzerland has no exploitable mineral resources, and its industries such as foundries in the Jura region and aluminium refining and smelting in the Valais also rely on electricity. Energy in the form of oil and gas has to be imported, and recently even much of the electricity in the drier season has been bought from other countries, notably France with its massive nuclear power resources. Switzerland produces a little nuclear power of its own, but the generators are nearing the end of their life and the country is facing up to their decommissioning before even thinking about a new generation of power stations.

Wood is very intelligently exploited here—forest management and regeneration is a fine art. The Swiss are pushing the boundaries of its potential as both a construction material and—with the price of oil rising—an important fuel for heating.

The country boasts no really major city in the world sense. The biggest city, Zürich, with a population of just over a million, does not even figure in the city league table of our atlas; that said, it has considerable resonance in the world of international banking and in culture. Basel and Geneva, each around the 500,000 mark, if looked at in their regional contexts also have a wider reputation—the former in international pharmaceutics, the latter with its United Nations affiliations and banking and watchmaking industries. Other Swiss cities such as Bern (the federal capital), Lausanne and St Gallen have between 200,000 and 350,000 people, and are all quietly, albeit proudly, provincial in comparison.

All the main urban centres have excellent educational facilities, and Switzerland boasts 10 state universities and two federal institutes of technology, as well as an extensive higher education network of technical, commercial, art and agricultural schools.

Most Swiss work in the tertiary sector nowadays, with massive employment in the banking, transport and communication industries. There is also a good section of the population in the manufacturing sector—those industries that make Switzerland famous and prosperous, notably watches, electrical goods and certain foods. The graphic arts and printing sectors (both manufacturing and production) have an enviable reputation here, but much of the know-how is now worldwide in these fields. Farming and forestry, although important, are relatively modest employers; as elsewhere, footwear and textile production have moved to countries with lower labour costs.

For historical reasons Switzerland has sourced much of its labour force in other countries by immigration. Currently, about a third of the population is made up of foreign nationals. Most of the people living here see this

Switzerland is home to migrants from neighbouring countries as well as those from further afield such as this lady from Albania.

as a source of strength in diversity, although as in other European countries some political parties are prepared to wheel out racist and xenophobic garbage at election time. A popular vote last year—whipped up by the populist xenophobes—was passed prohibiting the erection of minarets in Switzerland. Local building codes and consent regulations already permitted the contestation of buildings on a case-by-case basis. Well, if Switzerland wants to look a fool in the world's eyes....

So the political climate is not that different from the rest of Europe. Nor is the meteorological one, which runs from pretty hot to pretty cool. These days it tends to get pretty hot for a few weeks in summer, peaking in the low- or even mid-thirties (around 90°F) in July/August. In the mountains it is, naturally, cooler, and if you don't like strong heat, it can be very pleasant in a mountain village in summer. In winter, of course, it gets seriously cold there. Temperatures can easily go down to –12°C (10.4°F) or even –20°C (–4°F) in mountain villages at night, with lashings of snow. Down in the valleys, it's a little warmer certainly, but with the wind and sleet and sub-zero readings—frequently as low as –10°C (14°F)—it's nice to be indoors then.

THE MYTH OF CLEANLINESS

One of the myths one used to hear talked about was that Switzerland was somehow cleaner than elsewhere. The rest of the world was rather grubby while the Swiss were squeaky clean. Like most myths this one needs clarification to get away from a *Heidi* reading of a 'hygienist' alpine paradise. In reality, Switzerland is much on the same level as the other European countries I have visited. In fact, downtown Lisbon at one in the morning felt cleaner than downtown Zürich: fewer hamburger wrappers, dog turds and drink cans.

In the perpetuation of this myth, two factors are at play. First there is the history of tourism. The English came on their Grand Tours in the Enlightenment era of the late 18th and early 19th century, young gentlemen dropping in on de Haller, Voltaire, de Saussure or Rousseau, earnestly walking in the Alps on their quest of the sublime, taking the high and spectacular road between Germany or Geneva and Italy, lusting after the thick-ankled boat girls on Luzern's sparkling lake. These young gentlemen were used to the finer things in life and when they alighted on some huddle of hovels in the Alps they noisily brayed for a hot bath and clean sheets, spreading gold sovereigns around. So was born the highly lucrative trade of Swiss paying hospitality. From inns to more pretentious hotels, these sprang up along the mountain passes, in picturesque cities and by the side of peaceful lakes. All charged prices to match the young lords' ample allowances, and all had hot and cold running maids.

The rest of Switzerland, already pretty enough, launched

itself into a frenzy of beautification—geranium window boxes, picturesque fountains, everything was polished up for the market, and life became much more pleasant all round. A tourist economy, as most countries in the poorer or more beautiful parts of the world have found, can carry a small and energetic population quite sweetly. Historically this coincided with the rise of railway transport, which came rather late to Switzerland with its difficult terrain but which made (and still makes) train travel here a spectacular experience. The endless series of tunnels and viaducts giving views of truly breathtaking landscapes. The thing obviously snowballed, and the capacity of Switzerland to welcome well-heeled travellers seemed unlimited.

The second factor was the fact that Switzerland, unlike its neighbours, had no coal. The country was spared the horrendous pollution that heavy industry and mining inflicted on other European countries—Belgium, northern France, Germany, Britain. This kept the air reasonably clear, with energy coming from the ample hydro-electricity produced from the inexhaustible supply of melting snow.

All this helped to give Switzerland its salubrious and health-giving reputation. Sanatoriums sprang up to treat the symptoms of various pulmonary conditions, of which tuberculosis was the best known. In the 20th century a whole school of thought labelled 'Hygienism' sprang up which affected housing, education and sanitation. Switzerland was at the forefront of this movement and the comparative smallness of its urban centres allowed it to create quite spectacular urban projects, from garden suburbs and worker cities to the satellite cities of the post-WWII era that were usually connected to centres by non-polluting electrified bus or rail lines.

Of course the rise of the motor car, which reached a crisis level in the last decades of the 20th century, took its toll on the legendary cleanness of the air. The densification of cities led to the usual mix of air and noise pollution with which most cities around the world are familiar. So, behind the squeaky clean surfaces Switzerland is not significantly cleaner than

The town of Zermatt does not allow cars in. Welcome to a quiet and unpolluted place.

Although graffiti is frowned upon, it still exists in the country.

its neighbours, although to its credit it has started treating these problems with considerable energy, much as the rest of Europe is doing. Non-polluting transport infrastructures are being reinstated at great expense, the elimination of rubbish of various forms is a major political and engineering priority, and kids are being reprimanded when caught spraying obscenities on the dignified walls of public edifices.

Do as the Locals Do

As far as you are concerned, dear reader, the world is more pleasant and comfortable if you obey the various suggestions, exhortations and laws which will make the country a cleaner place for us all. Sorting out garbage into glass, paper, tin cans and organic becomes an easy routine quite quickly, and you will learn where the nearest carwash is (to avoid polluting the stormwater drains) and all of the other little services which you will find in most places.

Rules that defy common sense are usually dropped quite quickly. Ten years ago some earnest soul discovered that idling car engines gave out large amounts of carbon monoxide and other toxic gases, and it was decreed that all cars should turn their engines off at traffic lights while waiting for them to turn green. This brilliant and sincerely applied idea, which had policemen blowing their whistles at Fiats spluttering away at downtown intersections, was discreetly dropped when other scientists pointed out that even more severe pollution was caused by the unburned gases spewed out when a hundred starters whirred and whinnied in unison. Since then cars with fuel injection and catalytic exhaust systems have helped a little in making emissions cleaner. The considerable hike in fuel prices in recent times has furthermore driven many Swiss to use their excellent public transport systems and leave their cars at home.

So the air has become a bit better, and in most Swiss

The efficient Swiss public transport system integrates the various modes of travel to provide seamless passage.

centres spectacular publicly funded urban transport schemes are mushrooming and moving thousands of people around in clean and pleasant conditions.

The Zürich S-Bahn is the most impressive result so far. Co-financed by the Federal Railways and the regional authorities, it stretches over a huge catchment region with underground and existing lines integrated. Sexy new rolling stock assures high frequencies of passage at peak hours, and you can still get home to your suburb after a Wagner opera or a rave party in the city. The people one sees on board seem proud of their trains, well-versed in the mysteries of the system, and always happy to tell you which line goes where and exactly when. Figures show that in greater Zürich 20 per cent of people use the S-Bahn, and 37 per cent of commuters use public transport.

Traffic pollution aside, there is another kind of dirt in Switzerland—more insidious, more dangerous and politically more difficult to handle. This is the spectacular residue of industrial pollution. Scratch the ground in the sinister zone at the entrance to Basel, where the huge chemical firms have been installed for a good century, and you will find deposits of heavy metals, organic pollutants and other horrors quietly seeping into the river Rhine as it flows out of Switzerland to pollute Germany, France and the Netherlands. Direct water contamination is no longer a major issue, barring accidents—I have seen thousands of dead fish in the stream next to where I live as the result of a 'human error' in an industrial plant 10 km (6.21 miles) upstream—but the ground is proving very difficult to clean up and the situation is a major public-health concern. Cantons are drawing up pollution ground maps with traces of chemicals and their possible nature carefully represented, but there's years of work to do yet to get the place clean again.

Nor has Switzerland, with a very small and dwindling nuclear power base, come anywhere near to a solution to eliminating nuclear waste, but this as well as the chemical one is a problem they share with most of the developed world.

HISTORY IN 5 EASY SECTIONS
Some Prehistory and Early Stuff

Research is still going on into the prehistory of central Europe. To simplify matters considerably, we can imagine Switzerland long before it existed as mountains and swamps with settlements of Celts and other short folk who probably lived on houses built over the water or mud—not unlike the longhouses found in parts of Asia—or as hill tribes living in various forms of caves and wrapped in bear furs for a little warmth.

One can visualise settlements by some of the lakes and rivers at the time of Julius Caesar, who came marching through the land of the Helvetians and the Allobrogians on his way north around 50 BC with his men, all in their helmets and sexy tunics. As Romans will, they arranged a few things, bridged the Rhone in Geneva, built a few comfortable villas with lake views, and a pretty impressive bath and sports complex up in the Windisch Baden region. They also found and cleared some nice slopes and planted vines there. In the Tyrol region and what is now the Grisons they found large deposits of salt. The salt mines of Bex, at the head of Lake Geneva, are operating to this day and are well worth a visit.

The Devil's Bridge spans the narrow but treacherous Reuss River below. There has been a bridge at this strategic site since the 12th century.

A number of cities were founded in the later Roman period, when settlement and trade became important. Although much was swept away during the violent period of the 3rd and 4th centuries, archaeologists have made some impressive discoveries in the last few decades, enriching our knowledge of that period considerably.

The Burgundians—derived from the Celtic tribes—and a Germanic people called the Allemannians, drifted in from the west and north respectively during this period. They seem to have created new settlements outside the older towns, many of which later became towns. Their settlement patterns go some way in explaining the linguistic divide between the German-speaking and the French-speaking parts of the present country.

Christianity was introduced around 720 AD by Irish monks, the best-known of whom, Gallus, settled near what later became the city of St Gallen. As elsewhere in the region, the monks' influence was instrumental in the creation of a literate administrative class, and in the considerable improvements in farming technology (crop rotation), architecture and business practice. St Gallen still has Switzerland's most important school of business. The clerics also brought in books and set up a very important library—which exists to this day and houses a priceless collection of medieval manuscripts. The various bishops in the cities and abbots further afield laid claim to vast tracts of land and certain cities, making them into fortified citadels, and laid a network of roads and ways through the country. Some spectacular routes that are now walking paths date from that period—notably the Alpine crossings in the Uri Gotthardt region (central Switzerland), which constituted the ancient north-south route linking Lombardy and Germany—and come complete with tollgates, inns and relays. The Devil's Bridge (Teufelsbrücke), which in its first form dates from the 12th century, is one of the most magnificent vestiges of these old roads.

At this point, there was still no Swiss state to speak of as such. At the very most, it was a Helvetian region with a few paths, a few abbeys and fortified cities, and a population of perhaps a quarter of a million speaking some form of German, and Old French further west. Charlemagne was perhaps the first secular ruler of the region when he was crowned Emperor by the Pope in 800 AD, but his sons split the region up and quickly lost control. This is where the Hapsburgs, who had holdings in the northeast of the region and also in what is now Austria, stepped in and became the rulers of much of the region. In fact, they had their headquarters in what is now the canton of Aargau, which slopes down towards the Rhine in the northwest present-day Switzerland. They laid claim to parts of the territory in the 8th to 10th century, and subsequently spotted the place with some spectacular castles (many of which are still there today), although they were rarely able to impose their rule in any real way outside of their fortresses. Like all mountain peasants, the old Swiss were a truculent bunch.

Telling It Like It Is—1291 and All That

I hate to 'Tell' you this but the apple business appears to have no historical foundation. The origins of Switzerland are based on rather more mundane, although still interesting, premises.

The modern nation is rooted in the creation of a number of important centres—Bern, Luzern and Zürich—all of which became powerful in the 11th and 12th centuries, with trade and merchants' guilds and a considerable secular hold on their hinterlands. Most significantly, their growth was stimulated by the opening of a pass through the Göschenen Valley, which enabled lucrative trade to be carried over from Lombardy and Valais. The region thus served as a series of staging posts on the vital north-south trade route, with the lakes of Luzern and Zurich used for navigation. For the Hapsburgs, these centres were highly strategic, allowing them to administer their own fiefs in the valleys of Schwytz and Uri under royal patronage, with treaties signed from 1230 to 1240. These valleys were now important trade routes. The story goes that in 1291, on the death of the Hapsburg king, the peasants swore on the field of Rütli in Uri to oppose any attempts by a future Hapsburg

nobleman to assert his authority over them. This was in fact a declaration of independence, and their alliance was sealed by a document called the Act of Confederation. This act, one of the sacred documents of the Swiss federal state, still exists in the national archives. The gathering on the field is undocumented, but not improbable, as the primitive Swiss, in common with other Nordic peoples, had a tradition of solving issues by public meetings and voting by a show of hands.

The William Tell story is less probable, to put it mildly. It seems to originate in a 16th-century popular ballad, published at a time when by various vagaries of history the confederation of Swiss states had grown to 13 cantons and had become pretty assertive, their expansion arrested only after they lost the battle of Marignano in 1513 against French troops. The story, which was published in various versions in the subsequent century, began to create an iconography of some importance. The German Romantic poet and friend of Goethe, Friederich Schiller, came across it at the end of the 18th century, when Switzerland was the 'Helvetic Republic', a rather odd revolutionary state that Napoleon created to avoid having to bother with a total military conquest of a difficult and truculent land. During this period the Tell myth, of the heroic lowly-born individual creating an egalitarian and democratic state, had spread beyond the borders of the small country. Schiller's 1805 play is a splendid Byronic work in the Romantic idiom of the day, set in thumping blank verse, and is still enthusiastically performed in Attinghausen every summer, with the backdrop of the beautiful mountains of four cantons coming down to the lake.

Strife and Unity, from the Reformation to the Founding of a New Land

The subsequent history of Switzerland crosses paths with a number of currents. The Reformation was a spiritual and secular response to the complacency and corruption of the Catholic Church at the beginning of the 16th century, fomented by the advent of humanist and scholastic ideas. Erasmus worked in Basel, Luther's ideas were assiduously listened to by the Zürich scholar Zwingli, and another reformator, Guillaume Farel arrived in Geneva and worked with John Calvin to form a very puritanical Protestant civic doctrine based on the idea of predestination. This happened at a time when communication between European centres was on the increase, when commercial and military sciences were in evolution, and when literacy and basic learning were becoming important among a larger sector of the population, above all in the cities. As much of the movement was north-south, Switzerland was effectively at the centre of it; its model of government began to interest certain currents in the southern and northern states between which the voyagers travelled.

Switzerland would have its religious wars in the 16th century, with the periphery and Zürich embracing Protestantism, and the central cantons reinforcing their militant Catholicism and setting up important Counter-Reformation centres such as the Baroque Jesuit Centre in Luzern and the Monastery of Einsiedeln in the central mountains. This period and the 17th century were also the peak periods of young Swiss serving as mercenaries on various sides in the endless wars of Italy, Germany and France.

The Thirty Years' War (1618–1648) passed Switzerland by, but drained thousands of men in its senseless bloodshed. Swiss peasants were poor, and there was not usually room on the land for more than one or two sons. So the others would ride off as mercenaries on fine Swiss warhorses (also very much in demand it seems) to Milan, Rome, Konstanz or Avignon to join various princes, kings or bishops in their war campaigns. Many would die, of course, as often of diseases as of battle wounds. Others would come back with some money eventually, but above all with precious acquired know-how, a language here, a trade there, information on a new route, friends in high places. They would also inevitably bring back military skills, thereby occasionally escalating the erstwhile squabbles between Protestant and Catholic cantons or cities into pitched battles.

The next pattern of Swiss expansion was essentially one of the annexation of land by the rich cities or occasionally bishoprics of the countryside around them. So, for example, Aargau (the fief on the river Aare) and Thurgau (likewise on the river Thur) became the subject lands (and hunting grounds) of the gentry of Bern and Zurich. The hinterlands of the city of St Gallen annexed by the bishop formed the future canton of St Gallen during this state's Catholic era.

Switzerland had declared itself an independent and neutral federal republic in 1649 in the receding shadow of the wars. But it would not be appropriate or right to call it a democracy as it stood then. Rule was by oligarchies in the prosperous cities of the poorer citizens and the humble peasants in the countryside. A number of revolts attempted by these latter, or the lower orders in the cities in the 17th and 18th century, were more or less brutally put down.

It took the idealism of the Age of Enlightenment to forge Switzerland in the model to

Maths Whiz

Famous mathematicians of the day—like John Bernoulli (1667–1748), his son Daniel Bernoulli (1700–1782) and Leonard Euler (1708–1783)—established Basel as an important centre progressive mathematical theory.

which we have become accustomed. The catalyst for this was the liberation of much of the country by the young and much-admired Napoleon, with his republican troops. Switzerland, based above all on several urban centres, was in intellectual and political ferment. Its writers, savants and many exiles from other countries began to be heard internationally. Horace Bénedict de Saussure (1740–1799), the Genevan, is best known as the conqueror of Mont Blanc, but his scientific and theoretical writings also put Geneva (then an independent republic) on the map. Voltaire had a house in Geneva, and a castle in France across the border, where he wrote his brilliant, corrosive satires. With typical elegance he had a garden which straddled the French-Genevan border. Thus when French soldiers came to arrest him for sedition or blasphemy or whatever, he simply strolled across the border into rapid exile. His turbulent friend, Jean Jacques Rousseau (1712–1785), a Genevan watchmaker by trade, began to systematise ideas of the freedom of the individual in the context of a democratic state (*The Social Contract*, 1762). He spent most of his life in France, where his posthumous influence was vital in moulding the republican form the state would take after 1789.

When the French stormed the Bastille and the Revolution began in earnest, there was one incident at the Tuileries Palace where a company of 800 Swiss mercenaries was massacred by the crowds. This tragic event would likely have set the people in an increasingly educated Switzerland thinking about the utility of doing the dirty work for corrupt monarchies.

It was ideas like these that Bonaparte, the young Corsican general, had in his baggage when he set out to 'liberate' Europe in the name of Enlightenment. In fact he was invited into Switzerland by the people of the canton of Vaud, who had been under the yoke of Bern for nearly a century. They had launched a war of revolt against Bern in 1795 and boldly declared a République de Léman (Lake Geneva's French name) with their neighbours, and were pleased when Napoleon's troops who had annexed Geneva and a large chunk of the west of Switzerland marched triumphantly up through Bern and Zürich. The Helvetic

Republic was declared with considerable enthusiasm in 1798, and it led to the resignation or ousting of a number of corrupt and oligarchic governments, notably in Luzern and Fribourg. It also freed the territories of the Valais and Thurgau in the north-east, both of which eventually became rural cantons.

What soon caused trouble was the French obsession with central government. The central Swiss states, reactionary Catholics, as well as the remoter valleys of the Grisons, never really accepted this state of affairs, and went on having their assemblies and doing everything possible to prevent the centralised system from being operational. Worse, Switzerland became a theatre of war, with battles fought between Austrian and French troops, and thus suffering the whole catastrophe of military occupation, the foraging and billeting of troops, and the exactions on city and country finances. Moreover no one could ignore the dictatorial tendencies in the later phases of Napoleonic France. The fear that gripped the Swiss was real.

From 1812 to 1814, Napoleon's troops finally retreated. In the context of the peace of Vienna, the boundaries of Switzerland were fixed—in which state they largely remain today—and its status as a neutral and non-belligerent state was confirmed.

This, alas, meant that in parts of the country the oligarchies were re-established. The fight between (mainly Catholic) conservatives in the central cantons and more liberal elements actually led to a brief civil war when the former declared a separate confederacy (Sonderbund) in 1847 and raised an army with help promised from the Austrian emperor and the Russian tsar. The liberal states rapidly counter-attacked, and were fortunate in finding a brilliant general who had been educated in France, the Genevan Guillaume-Henri Dufour. His knowledge of topography, military acumen and political sensibility were extraordinary, and the war was over within a month, with only 86 casualties. Dufour was one of Henri Dunant's friends and was subsequently instrumental in the founding of the Red Cross.

In 1848, the first federal constitution was adopted.

It took, however, years of acrimonious squabbling and another constitution in 1872 to get a true democratic federal Switzerland—defining the place of central and state governments—running on all cylinders.

Smokestacks, Waterspouts and Red Scares (1872–1931)

Switzerland is not known for its natural resources. The industry that existed helped refine raw materials and added considerable value to it by manual or industrial intervention.

One of the first cottage industries that Switzerland knew—going back to the Middle Ages—was the spinning, weaving and embroidery of textiles. The St Gallen and Appenzell regions in the north-eastern hills were the best known for this, although my mother speaks affectionately of a white-bearded grandfather in Thurgovie who did lacemaking piecework until his eyesight failed and ended up as a village night watchman. One assumes he still had enough sight to spot whatever heinous crimes you might find in a village of 200 souls, 20 cows and 17 apple trees.

In the 19th century, industrial textile works rapidly gained importance. The city of St Gallen had imported its first state-of-the-art machines, of English manufacture, in 1801. They used water power, as Switzerland had no coal resources. It seems that by the time of the Treaty of Vienna (1816), the textile industry was completely mechanised, with large clattering factories mushrooming, though one assumes without the pall of smoke that Engels was to see in England a few decades later.

It seems natural that dyes with carefully controlled colour and stability qualities would be required in large quantities, and the burgeoning Swiss chemical industry had its origin in this period also. Ciba in Basel started production in 1859 and became Ciba Geigy in the 1880s. Synthetic pharmaceutical production started at around the same time, with Sandoz and Hoffman de la Roche, also in Basel, raising their retorts and smokestacks.

It was quickly established that machinery could be better produced locally than imported at great expense from

England. Pioneers in this field were Sulzer and Escher-Wyss in the Zurich region and Charmilles in Geneva. The former was soon building major spinning and textile machines, while the latter were important in the field of hydraulic energy conversion and the turbines that would soon give Switzerland its international reputation as a producer of hydro-power and an exporter of machinery.

From 1857, Geneva had a high-pressure water network along the Rhône which drove small water-powered machines for the watch industry, as well as chocolate grinders. The city's famous water jet is a vestige from this era, as the surplus pressure spouted up as a fountain in the evenings when the factories turned off their taps.

Switzerland in the 19th and early 20th centuries was as affected as the rest of Europe by demographic changes and urban expansion. Cities like Zürich, St Gallen, Winterthur and Baden found their populations increasing enormously. Much work was done on the creation of new housing, usually of a reasonable quality, and for the infrastructure of engineering and transport that was inevitable as a base for all that. A foundry in Schaffhausen, Georg Fischer, started producing pipes and components for water and gas, establishing standards in that field.

For transport, a railway network was built, initially in a piecemeal way, but soon with a normalisation of gauges (rail width and wagon profiles for tunnels and bridges) to avoid the pitfalls seen in England and elsewhere 50 years earlier. Switzerland quickly started producing its own rolling material and electric locomotives, trams and trolleybuses.

Automobile production was never important. The legendary Pic Pic (how could they hope to market such a ridiculous name?) in Geneva ceased production in WWI or during the Depression. Saurer in Arbon, just across from Germany, continued building diesel-powered trucks until the eighties; they had been in touch with Rudolph Diesel from 1908 and on the oil engine's inventor's untimely death in 1913, they kept the patents for his brilliant motors. After this, for five decades, Saurer got a small royalty payment for every diesel motor produced in the world. The world wars led to vast income for this small plant in a neutral land. Alas, when this income petered out, the company quietly went to the wall.

Labour means a certain amount of legislation, and also labour unions. We have a photo of our old grandfather, a toolmaker, at the socialist Second International, in Bâle in 1912. A tough young man in shirtsleeves, the archetypal worker, ardent reader of George Bernard Shaw, he is flanked by two men in jackets and hats. Legislation to make work bearable came very slowly in this part of the world. The first child-labour laws in Zürich in 1815 limited the working day of 10-year-olds to 12 hours a day! By the end of the century a federal law restricted work to people over the age of 14 and a reasonable system of compulsory universal education was in place throughout the land.

There were unions, there were strikes. One of the worst was the general strike of 1918, when Switzerland was coming out of a long and harsh period of precarious unity frozen by the threat from all around it. What workers demanded seems reasonable to us now: a 48-hour week, stricter labour safety legislation, and votes for women. Predictably the authorities moved in with the army and the strike was brutally broken. A similar confrontation in Geneva in November 1931 resulted in Swiss soldiers shooting 11 demonstrators.

World War II: Before, During and After
In the 20th century—and above all in the aftermath of the Wall Street crash—Switzerland knew poverty again, as well as fear and the concomitant political agitation. Political movements both on the extreme left and on the nationalistic right sprung up. Wedged as it was between the two brassy Fascist states of Germany and Italy, Switzerland witnessed emulative movements towards a Fascist or National Socialist state structure, movements which, along with a vigorous Moscow-oriented Communist Party, would create tension during World War II. Many Swiss intellectuals and professionals emigrated, some to America, others to Soviet Russia. There was also a sizeable emigration movement among the poorer folk, such as farmers, who set out to begin

new lives in Australia, Canada, Africa and South America. These migrant communities have often formed cohesive unities in their adopted homelands: we know of a Helvetia in Brazil, and of a whole region of Swiss dairy farmers in the Taranaki region of New Zealand who established themselves in that period.

The Second World War was a difficult period for Switzerland, which defended itself by means of a National Redoubt in its mountainous central region, and a scorched-earth policy for the border and lowlands. Switzerland had a visionary military leader in General Henri Guisan, but he was occasionally as much at war with defeatist and frankly pro-Fascist local elements as with any imagined threat from outside the national borders. As I mention in my discusson on banks, there were other major reasons why the Axis powers did not bother rolling their tanks into Switzerland. Sealed trains went from Italy to Germany and back through the country at night containing goods and probably people. This shadowy area is now being investigated by a new generation of historians but, as elsewhere in the world, sorting out the less honourable aspects of national policy is always a difficult battle.

Certainly no one can deny that Swiss armament and precision manufacturers and the big international firms had a pretty glorious war in terms of the profit made from both sides. British ships had Oerlikon anti-aircraft batteries, and truck manufacturer Saurer's name is linked with the darker pages of the Nuremberg trials and the Holocaust.

During this period a huge movement made Switzerland as close to independent as possible in terms of its needs. The Wahlen Plan, named after a federal councillor, turned public parks into carrot and cabbage patches. Methods of gas production using Switzerland's ample wood supply were experimented with and a fairly strict rationing policy was introduced for indispensable food and other supplies. The country was not generous in its admission of foreign refugees on the other hand: people of Jewish descent could have a 'J' stamped in their passports even before the outbreak of hostilities.

Switzerland emerged from the war pretty much unscathed—compared to the destruction around it. The one bombing incident in 1945 involved the city of Schaffhausen, where the Americans dropped a few stray bombs, resulting in more than a hundred deaths. Nevertheless Switzerland was able to be of some help in patching up the infrastructure of neighbouring countries, and the Geneva-based Red Cross redoubled its efforts to repatriate those displaced by the war.

The League of Nations in Geneva, which had failed to prevent the carnage of the Second World War, was revived, and Geneva became the headquarters of the United Nations Organisation, the non-political conference centre of that fine political institution. It has also since become the world headquarters of half a dozen other important specialised UN bureaux, the best known of which are the World Health Organisation, the International High Commission for Refugees and the International Labour Office.

Locally Switzerland finally voted and institutionalised some much-needed social laws, assuring an old-age and disability benefit for all, legalising the complex dossiers of public health care and setting up a federal network of higher technical education.

This was again a period of vast urban renewal that saw the creation of huge suburban dormitory cities on Hygienist principles, in an attempt to relieve the density of city centres. Much damage was done during this period, however, by ill-considered public works and private projects. Fortunately, the pendulum now seems to be swinging—albeit timidly—back to a policy of conservation and the maintenance of an urban population.

Switzerland Now

It is difficult to write about the last few decades without sounding slightly sententious or a wee bit pompous, yet Switzerland is as much a little paper boat navigating in the currents of the history of our planet as any other place and we must try.

So, to start at the end, Switzerland is slowly but surely being hauled into the collective world of modern Europe, and that has probably been the salient issue of the debates of the last two decades. It has given rise to an isolationist position with the profiling of a right-wing group (the Swiss People's Party, or UDC), which looks with fear and loathing on the prospect of Swiss traditions being lost in the morass of European bureaucracy. A similar point of view is expressed by a part of the left of the political spectrum, which sees the new Europe as a gigantic plot being hatched by *laissez faire* liberalism with the privatisation and buying out of the public sector economy as a pretty public agenda. Events in Portugal and, above all, Greece—where local financial sloppiness is meeting the greed of the Euro-bankers and sending the populace into the streets—may justify this. Certainly the Swiss are less than comfortable with an overly rapid homogenisation of our nation into the Europe of which it is part, and this fear is reflected by the rather patchy plebiscites of pro-European initiatives by popular vote. A full-scale adhesion to the European economic space, although voted for by a majority in a 2004 plebiscite, was lost on the technicality that a majority of (often tiny) cantons was against it. On the other hand, the citizens of Switzerland finally voted to join the UN as a full member in 2002, albeit by a narrow majority after a long and often bitter debate. Opposition by the right to allow Swiss peacekeeping troops to be armed was also narrowly defeated by a popular vote.

The Swiss system of voting on most issues has been at once a source of direct democracy and incredible delay in political decisions. But on the whole it has generally meant that any decision that the majority has voted for is usually respected nationally (or at a state level in the case of state votes) and implemented with a certain degree of consideration for the minority view whenever possible.

An exception has been the application of a draconian and xenophobic policy against refugees on Swiss soil, which the now disgraced Minister of the Interior decreed in 2006. The more progressive cities and states have quite simply refused to take the measures demanded, on humanitarian—though more often pragmatic—grounds. Sometimes the very cumbersome political system works in favour of slowing a change or a tendency that may do harm. Switzerland always seems to be a decade behind others.

The kind of problem the slow Swiss run into was graphically illustrated with the disastrous organisation of the national exposition that was initially billed as Swissexpo 2001 but which eventually had to be hastily and rather embarrassingly renamed Swissexpo 2002 when it became obvious that the financing and infrastructure work were simply not up-to-date.

The Swiss nation plods on regardless, primarily I suspect because its national identity is worn so lightly. At the Seville International Fair a decade before the Swiss one, one of the slogans was *'La Suisse n'existe pas'* ('Switzerland doesn't exist'), where the ontological existence of the little pink navel in the centre of a blue Europe was simply denied. We became a kind of non-entity, and navel-gazing is definitely

a national pastime. This non-identity would actually be logical if we take the history of Switzerland into account with its patchwork of different linguistic, cultural and religious traditions, so many sacred cows sitting in the village square and slowing the juggernaut of progress which has created and destroyed so much elsewhere.

Certainly Switzerland is opening up. An extension of the free exchange agreements we entered into with the rest of Europe is now in force, despite a few misgivings we all share and which are expressed on the fringes of our political spectrum. For most of us Europe is very much a future goal, albeit a Europe which will have to take us into account and respect the traditions and institutions which make the country what it is. By its regional position as much as by its considerable economic clout, Switzerland is getting and will go on getting a good hearing in Strasbourg and Brussels, and should be able to make a realistic contribution to the institutional and constitutional changes Europe is struggling with at the moment.

One does suspect, though, that much of Switzerland will go on as it has, a quiet picturesque backwater of polite and unpretentious people, a little slow to move and rather traditional, a relief to the bustle of what goes on all around it.

That is what the Swiss are good at. They seem to have been listening—through the news, the Internet and of course travel—to what the rest of the world is up to and up against, and quietly moving to make things work. The banks have cleaned up their act; in any case, with Internet banking and currency reforms, money stashed in a Zurich vault is no longer such a safe bet. The Swiss also seem to be quietly active on the diplomatic front, using their tradition of neutrality as a trump card in world affairs. So during the US–Iran hostage crisis in 1979, the Swiss embassy in Teheran was quietly in charge of US affairs and presentation. The Swiss are one of the major sponsors of the Palestine-Israel peace initiative. Their efforts are so far falling on deaf ears, but an institutional and legal network is being put into place behind the scenes, involving a number of countries and representatives of progressive people both in Israel and Palestine.

On another level Switzerland, along with their big northern neighbour Germany, has been doing a lot of work and research in the field of sustainable development of resources. They have an interest in this, as Switzerland is at the source of much of western Europe's water, with the Rhine and the Rhône both rising in the Swiss Alps. Much work has also been done on wood; and forestry management in terms of a long-term resource is a major preoccupation of local industry and research. Everything from very large wooden structures in aircraft hangars and sports halls to the use of wood pellets as a fuel in the hard winters is being researched and commercialised. Visitors come from all over the world to see the progress being made in the use of this resource by a small country.

Sustainable Work

A forester I know who works in the municipal forests of Lausanne spends two months every year in Pakistan working on a major reforestation project. He is funded by the federal government. Another friend has a lively exchange going introducing organic market gardening into a region of Senegal, and is learning a great deal as he goes. Exchanges always work two ways.

A PEASANT CONFEDERACY

Switzerland owes its tradition of democratic rule to its origins, as a series of isolated small entities—often scarcely more than villages—which the locals had more or less taken over from duchies, bishoprics and other administrative systems that had collapsed, or given up, under the weight of time.

Collective action came naturally in a hostile and merciless environment, where neighbourly help in the herding of cattle, opening of paths, management of forests and occasionally defence against marauders or foreign armies was part of a way of life. Very often the power was in the hands of nearby cities, or locally vested in one or more families a little richer, luckier and more cunning than those around them, but large feudal estates are simply not a practical possibility in a land so chopped up by mountains, valleys and waterways. To quote from a very well-documented website:

Many people are inclined to believe that Switzerland is the most ancient democracy in the world. But this is only a partial truth. Consider the period of the so-called Helvetic Republic— Napoleon's creation in 1798:

1. *The small rural districts in central Switzerland (Uri, Schwyz, Unterwalden, Glarus) and Appenzell had a primitive form of direct democracy called 'Landsgemeinden'. All male citizens would meet regularly to elect the government and decide important matters. But effectively a small number of rich families were represented in the government and prepared the political agenda and the decisions.*

2. *The citizens of the cities had the right to elect the city councils, but only members of a small number of families were eligible, be it in the form of patrician oligarchy (Bern, Solothurn, Fribourg, Lucerne) or in the form of guilds of master craftsmen (Zurich, Basel, Schaffhausen).*

3. *A broad majority of the Swiss people—the peasants of the areas controlled by the cities of Zurich, Bern, Lucerne, Zug, Fribourg, Solothurn, Basel and Schaffhausen as well as the inhabitants of the subject territories under common administration by all member states of the old Swiss confederacy (Aargau, Thurgau, Vaud)—had no political rights.*

4. *Liberty of commerce and liberty of press were unknown in Switzerland just as in other countries.*

For women—not highly valued interlocutors in a peasant or traditional urban circle—voting and representation came scandalously late. It was finally granted by a popular vote instituting a constitutional change in 1971 after a great deal of rather dishonourable and acrimonious debate. The first woman entered the federal cabinet in 1984 with the Justice and Interior portfolios, but was expelled under a cloud after warning her corrupt business lawyer husband of a pending enquiry about his financial finagling. Things have come some way since, and at present we actually have more women than men in the 7-member federal council, including the president and the vice-president for 2011.

Swiss voting laws

Let's look at Swiss voting laws, both on the issue level (in which Switzerland is something of a pioneer) and in elections (which are much like anywhere else).

Since 1971 all Swiss on the electoral roll are, in theory, consulted about issues of national importance involving changes to the constitution. In addition, a large-enough group of petitioners can ask for a new law to be challenged by popular vote. For this, 50,000 signatures have to be collected nationally in a delay of 100 days after the promulgation of the law. To initiate a new law, double that number of signatures is required, and the delay is 18 months from the publication of the project to the handing in of the 'Popular Initiative', as it is called. You will often see little tables set up in town squares or outside shopping malls, where citizens, or members of political groupings, invite you to sign an initiative for or a referendum against a law. As non-Swiss you will naturally not be allowed to sign, but by all means take an interest; it will give you a good insight into how the system works and get you discussing with people from the whole political spectrum.

One of the mysteries of national-level voting is that not only a popular majority, but also a majority of the cantons is required to initiate any major change. So a majority of (mainly urban) Swiss have been for Switzerland's integration into Europe for a decade, but the issue is blocked by a number of the deeply conservative cantons—which represent but 15 to 20 per cent of the population.

Similar rules apply, with smaller numbers of petitioners required, for state and municipal matters. The franchise, however, is often wider, as many municipalities include

The Swiss take their civil rights very seriously and are likely to hold rallies or organise petitions in the town square to state their point.

foreigners after a certain number of years of residence on the rolls. This gives a better consultation base in the major cities, where the 'foreign' population often makes up a quarter to a third, the grumblings of a few nationalist diehards notwithstanding. Foreigners do pay taxes in Switzerland, their children go to our schools, and they do more than their bit to keep the economy running. In 1991 the voting age was lowered from 20 to 18.

The Federal Level

The Swiss federal state is responsible for foreign relations, national policy making, defence and security, and a look into federal educational, cultural, social and health policy. It also looks at road planning, regional issues and keeps a close eye on two federally controlled corporations—the postal and railway services, which remain largely state-financed. There is an important federal supreme court which sits in Lausanne that is Switzerland's highest instance of justice.

The federal assembly's representatives are organised in a bicameral pattern not unlike that of the United States.

A National Council (Nationalrat) is Switzerland's House of Representatives—200 members based on a proportional representation of one councillor for every 36,000 citizens. They are elected by the cantons every four years, on a complicated proportional-representation system depending on their political parties. They are paid a modest annuity and a more substantial sum for each session or commission they attend. They can initiate laws which are then ratified by the Upper House and by the Federal Council. They also need to ratify laws that come to them from the other two instances.

Swiss Capital

The capital of Switzerland is the beautiful central city of Bern, where the federal chambers sit in an impressive early-20th-century Parliament House, and where some (but not all) of the federal departments are based. Distances are small enough to allow for a good deal of decentralisation.

Above them is a Senate (the Ständerat/Conseil des Etats), consisting of two members per canton (some of the cantons are half-cantons, so have only one member each), to make a total of 46 members. Here, the democratic base is rather more elastic: One councillor of a populous state like Zürich represents some 600,000 voters each, while his colleague from the canton of Uri has the same clout at house divisions with only 17,000 voters behind him. Thus the senate is, almost by definition, deeply conservative.

Senate and National Council elections are both on a four-year basis, and, again like in the US, the votes are alternated on a two-year cycle.

The Federal Council (Bundesrat) is a seven-person executive voted into power by the united federal chambers. The nominees are generally proposed by a political party, and the government is always based on a coalition of different political colours, which involves a certain amount of horse trading before they are presented and voted for.

Interestingly Switzerland has a rather weak presidential office. Each of the Federal Councillors takes turns to assume the largely ceremonial function for a 12-month period. This year (2011) the president is a Socialist; next year a People's Party representative should be stepping in.

The State and City Levels

State administrations are generally a single assembly, with cabinet-level power vested in a State Council that varies in number depending on the canton. Geneva, as a large canton in terms of population, has seven, with the ministries divided among them. They represent a pretty wide political spectrum from Socialists to Ecologists to Liberals to Centrists, and are elected by popular vote on a proportional and runoff system for four years. The president's office is rotating: last year it was a Green, this year a socialist.

The state parliament has 50–200 members (*députés*) elected on a four-year term by proportional representation and spanning the political spectrum. They rule through commissions, and policy is decided by a parliamentary majority, again subject to popular referendums if enough people can be found to disagree.

City administrations are on a pretty similar basis, with again an executive with the mayor as a rotating office, and a municipal council. In villages the mayor is a four-year posting with two or more associates and a council of about a dozen elected members to deliberate on questions of policy.

Understanding the System

The system both nationally and locally is pretty democratic— and pretty rigid in terms of major policy changes being difficult to implement, which makes Switzerland a rather slow land institutionally. Two problems have led to criticism of the system. Firstly, as one might expect, the agenda for popular votes is pretty much manipulated by those in power, who set the calendar and are certainly not prepared to rock the boat. If an issue not to their taste comes to a vote nationally or at state level they have enormous leverage in placing posters on hoardings, and buying various kinds of advertising time or arranging to have their people on national TV or radio.

Secondly, there is a secret mechanism in government

that does some more distasteful things without the knowledge of the people. The story which broke some years ago of the massive Jewish funds stolen by Nazi-Germans that the Swiss banks managed to salt away for half a century after the end of World War II only emerged because a junior bank employee got curious about some documents in a bin ready for shredding. Government is involved in this through an old-boy network involving the richest citizens, often the judiciary, a university network, and higher-ranking army officers in our amateur militia army. When all these close ranks, things become very difficult and occasionally dangerous for seekers of justice.

A recent example was the collapse of Switzerland's superb airline, Swissair, soon after its privatisation in 2001, where a similar old-boy network has so far managed to protect the more rapacious and unscrupulous men in higher management, who made a killing before offering themselves golden retirements. The press, quite assertive at first, gradually fell silent, and we were obliged to follow the scandal in good foreign papers like the *Financial Times* or *Le Monde*. The affair was finally tried in Dübendorff in 2007, and the result was outrageous: all the defendants were set free—and accorded an indemnity of 1.5 million Swiss francs for their pains.

Undoubtedly the very definition of Switzerland's institutional federal framework as a 'confederacy' might give us a hint towards an explanation.

Invisible Wealth

The Swiss have an odd relationship with their wealth.

On the one hand, Switzerland is definitely one of the richest countries of the world. It ranks fourth in terms of GDP per capita, and was recently placed second in the *Economist*'s Quality of Life index (a pretty complex formulation taking a raft of data on board including income, health, education, life expectancy, family life, climate, political stability, and so on). This also means that it is rather expensive for visitors, although as in all such standards the figures vary considerably depending on the region. So although Geneva and Zürich are costly, Paris, London and Hong Kong rank higher.

On the other hand, probably largely because the origins of its wealth are recent and always seem rather fragile, the Swiss seem to be chronically morose about the state of their economy, and are always predicting disasters around the corner. Switzerland, remember, has no minerals, no petroleum or gas, and a pretty forbidding if beautiful topography. Its industry is a toyshop compared to its neighbours France, Germany and Italy, not to speak of India or China or the US. Most of its know-how is, or was, imported from other countries. The Swiss banks were an Italian Renaissance invention; many of its financial institutions are based on British or Scottish ones. Even watchmaking came with the French Huguenots in the 17th century after the revocation of the Edict of Nantes, and the legendary Swiss railways are of course based on the British 19th-century invention of railway networks.

Swiss Power

The one major resource the Swiss have, and use very well, is hydro-electric power, but even there limits have been reached. Switzerland is also lumbered with two outdated and horrendously expensive giant nuclear power plants which they're trying to decommission.

The fact that the Swiss stubbornly hold on to their Swiss franc in the teeth of the Euro, which surrounds them, is no accident. Swiss products and services are far more expensive than their neighbours' and their salaries are very high, and somehow bankers seem to have a vision of the Swiss currency as a hedging fund against the instability of the Euro. Mostly, though, this turns out to be just a major local inconvenience.

Yes, there are the banks, of course, but even then they are pretty small fry compared to the big European, Asian or American houses. What they had, and what served them well in the 20th century, was a complete independence from government surveillance, allowing dubious money to be stocked here in numbered bank accounts and transactions to pass through Zürich from one shady dealer to another, leaving a nice little fee behind.

In the last decade, however, as the Philippines' Imelda Marcos and Nigeria's Abacha gang found out to their grief, this is no longer the case, and your nest egg can be revealed and eventually repatriated if your dictatorship comes to a messy end, as dictatorships often do. In our times, especially with our friends the Americans sticking their nose into every transaction, secret banking has become rather more difficult, if by no means impossible. If it's a question of a well-connected individual or firm salting away a few million for tax-evasion purposes the system is still pretty tight. But Swiss banks have to watch themselves when it comes to major mob money laundering or the funding of known terrorist groups, especially if these are on the American or Israeli hit lists. There are probably ways around this, but only your lawyer and your banker, cosily in bed with a national politician or two, would know for sure. The occasional news article, a politician's suicide, a banker found murdered, a government minister forced rather hurriedly to resign

for reasons of 'health' backs up a widely held suspicion of finagling. Nevertheless here, as elsewhere, the old-boy network is pretty inviolable.

The 1,000,000-Franc Suitcase

A story did the rounds some time ago, of a journalist from a prestigious Swiss weekly who one day went up and down Zurich's Bahnhofstrasse, where all of the great Swiss banks have their head offices, with an attaché case containing 1,000,000 Swiss francs in neatly bundled-up banknotes.

In bank after bank, he went up to the counter, opened his suitcase and asked what the bank suggested he do with his little nest egg. The story goes that, without exception, he was ushered into a back room and a banker came to consult with him about suitable kinds of investment accounts as well as other possibilities. The amazing thing was that not once in the ten or so establishments he visited was he asked, at the outset, his name, his nationality or where the money had come from. The Swiss institution of secret banking was inviolable—anything went and money was sacred.

In theory, things have now tightened up considerably. If you are a military dictator reading this book with a few millions of your people's money to stash away for a rainy day, you're probably entitled to open a Swiss account through the usual channels, but you will no longer be entitled to keep it secret. The Marcoses, Abachas, Papa Docs and others of this world have found this out at their considerable (albeit often posthumous) expense. It is more difficult to say what your treatment would be if you had a less high profile, although in the last couple of years, with a rather insistent American eye on larger transactions, I would certainly tread carefully before engaging in any funny business involving money. Notwithstanding, and without wanting to sound overly cynical, I would suspect that the larger the sum, the easier it would be to squirrel it away in one of the grey zones of the complex Swiss banking system.

If Switzerland still has a somewhat dubious reputation regarding trafficking of various kinds, involving drug money laundering, arms deals and other shady businesses, the federal laws have become far stricter and the banks have drawn up a pretty sound code of conduct. Looking at the newspapers (but then who owns the press?), it would seem that things have tightened and cleaned up considerably. Banking secrecy is still in the Swiss laws, but it is no longer quite what it was—for which, I suppose, we can be grateful.

But there are more good apples in the box than bad ones. The Swiss bankers I have dealt with have always been courteous, usually quite forthcoming with financial help, and very reliable. Interest rates, set by the banks and approved by a government organ, have usually been quite modest, often a couple of percentage points behind our neighbours. What this means, in fact, is that Switzerland has a very modest inflation rate. It makes Swiss investment funds a little slow-moving, although they should be pretty secure, give or take a few exceptions. So anyone who hadn't sold their shares in Swissair before that unfortunate company was ignominiously and disgracefully grounded in 2001 was either asleep or dead.

Swiss banks, about 400 of them altogether, come in all shapes and sizes. The Nationalbank in Bern holds Switzerland's still considerable gold reserves and is the country's monetary organ, instrumental in the setting of interest rates. It also issues Switzerland's very elegant banknotes. (Perhaps their aesthetic quality explains Switzerland's reluctance to embrace the somewhat drab Euro.) The national bank also has a beautifully constructed Internet site, which gives a clear exegesis of Swiss economic policy in all imaginable languages. The big sisters, UBS and Credit Suisse, have street-front agencies in every one-cow town, and offer the whole range of banking services. They were in the news with the scandal of vast amounts of gold stolen by the Nazis off Jews between 1930 to 1945 that had ended up in their coffers. If their initial reaction was rather less than honourable they appear to have come reasonably clean, and have kept an army of American lawyers rich and happy for a good decade now.

The Swiss National Post has a very efficient banking system which is poised to give complete services in the next year or two. They have the advantage of ubiquity. Despite strenuous efforts by management, Switzerland still has post offices in many villages where payments and transactions (Giros) are quickly and efficiently carried out for a minimal fee or free of charge. The cantonal banks were usually set up as state reserve banks in the last century. They have the advantage of proximity, and as a local businessman I dealt with the Geneva cantonal bank for three decades. Sometimes the proximity gets a little too cosy (see above under old-boy network). So another businessman whose hobbies were real estate speculation and asset stripping managed to take our bank to the cleaners for about a quarter of a billion Swiss francs. He'd put himself into a position where the size of his debt was such that the bank did not dare to foreclose his credit for fear of going to the wall themselves. He is now sitting in one of Switzerland's comfortable jails for a couple of years, and the bank has sold its old headquarters in the centre of Geneva to recover a few francs.

THE SWISS PEOPLE

CHAPTER 3

"Einstein disguised as Robin Hood."
—Bob Dylan

NATIONAL CHARACTERISTICS

It is very difficult to give a portrait of a people that does not slide off into caricature and become quickly dated and irrelevant. All the more so for the people of Switzerland—an entity that is, after all, a kind of compromise rather than a strong-centred nation. Think of a chocolate with a nice outer layer of hard chocolate. You bite into it and come to a soft centre which flows around in your mouth, a little oversweet; it worries the filling that's come loose in one of your back teeth. The substance of the thing was, after all, the delicious chocolate coating; the centre has melted away.

So it is with the nation of Switzerland. It was a tiny makeshift military alliance in its origins, grouped together to repel a greedy invader's attempts to civilise and organise them. (Looking at recent history elsewhere in the world, one can see that people are in general still pretty stubborn in not accepting what is regarded by others to be good for them; ask the Vietnamese, the Afghans or the Iraqis.) The thing grew like a snowball, taking on extra bits as time went by, usually more for reasons of convenience than of any deep-lying patriotism.

When patriotism was invented in the wake of Napoleon's invasion it led to a number of odd manifestations which lasted about a century, but it seems to most of us to be a bit outmoded nowadays. The Swiss would find the kind

Flag-waving in a show of patriotism during one of the local festivals.

A large number of the Swiss population is foreign, such as these Portuguese construction workers.

of patriotic rituals other countries engage in rather odd. Nowadays even the National Feast on 1 August is more an evening feast of good humour and neighbourliness than a demonstration of solemn love for one's country.

Pragmatism and self-interest, enlightened or not, are still rather important components of the Swiss national character inasmuch as such a thing exists. The conception of the Swiss as a hard-working, unimaginative little citizen, deeply conservative, with an eye on the cash register probably has some justification, and surfaces at occasional moments of irritation as you live here. Yet it is far from the whole picture, and I must insist yet again that a huge proportion of the Swiss population is either foreign or most definitely of foreign origin. As happens in any culture with a big immigration culture, the second generation immigrants are often almost caricatures of the perceived national character of their host country, which leads to a rather odd distortion in the myth of the national character. Some time back, for example, the mainstays of the right-wing patriotic party in Geneva were a first-generation Russian, some second-generation Italians and Spaniards, as well as a handful of Swiss-Germans and a Lebanese grocer.

Friendly Folks

You will often find your neighbours and friends here to be open-minded, sociable and sound folk, curious about your foreign origins. In general, they are well-travelled and well-educated enough to be at least moderately rounded and interesting. Take our first apartment in Geneva. The lady living below us was a lively college teacher from the Valais with a Turkish-Jewish boyfriend; the lady across from us was an international functionary, daughter of a Dutch NATO general (and a lousy cook); the couple next door were a smartass Cambodian student and his American college-teacher girlfriend; the lady just above us was a snappy journalist of Zürich origin with a somewhat neurotic Indian lover; and the nice man on the top floor was an Iranian economist. We are still good friends with two of them two decades later, and occasionally come across the others, whom we greet with pleasure.

Having said this, one characteristic we occasionally find irritating is a kind of bossiness—an urge to make you conform—which seems to be rather prevalent even among one's friends. One gets the feeling that your average Swiss always thinks that he knows best, and you know just as well that *you* actually know best. More vulgar folk will try to pull rank on you if you have a foreign accent or don't look exactly as they do. The more educated will do the same thing more subtly. The way around that one is essentially to do a dumb-foreigner act for their benefit and then go on quietly and confidently with what you have been doing all along.

If you are right, don't crow about it, what's the point? They are trying to be friendly. If you are wrong, learn the lesson (not necessarily they were right, but I made a mistake) and get on with other things. The dust will settle in time.

TOWNIES AND RURALS

Switzerland is rather unusual in that it has no really big cities. In terms of population and density even the biggest centre Zürich is just on a par with Hamilton, Ontario, or Omaha, Nebraska. Many Swiss live in small centres with populations ranging from about 7,000 to about 30,000. The reason for this is that distances are very small and lines of transport on the whole very good in the built-up part of the country. So, if you're a reasonably well-paid employee in Zurich you can live in a small village less than 50 km (31 miles) away and wake up to the sound of cowbells. Work could well be at most 45 minutes away—a short bicycle ride to the station and half-an-hour by train.

And in the smaller centres, there would be schools up to primary or junior-high level, a reasonable range of shops and services, a post office, a service station and some form of public transport connection. The place would almost certainly be a municipality, with an elected council and mayor, local *votations* and festivities. Many people would work locally or come from the region to work there in small industries or in an ever-decentralising tertiary sector. I know graphic designers, journalists and photographers who happily work from their homes in such places. (The Internet is a wonderful thing—endless attachments of work wafting all over the world.) They might go to the city once or twice a week to meet with clients or other interlocutors, or these people would

HE'S WORKING AT HOME TODAY

make it a short pleasure trip to come out and see them, for a change of air.

The old chasm that divided city slickers from country bumpkins has all but disappeared. When we go to concerts in the city we regularly run into farmer friends from the villages around, and the citizens of Lausanne flock to a summer theatre in a converted barn in a picturesque hillside village just 20 km (12.43 miles) from their city, where they gleefully pitch into local wine with little cheese-and-ham sandwiches after a good dose of Molière or Max Frisch.

If you want hostility you have to go inland and upwards. Go up onto the plateau behind the central lakes with foreign, or even out-of-state number plates on your car, and you'll catch certain members of the population peering at you. If you have the good fortune to have a skin tone other than pink they'll stare even more. They won't harm you but they'll have categorised you as bloody foreigners and their response to any question you might have will be terse, to put it mildly. We had Genevan number plates on our car, and I addressed someone in the village in the Swiss-German dialect and got a really frosty reaction—barely any eye contact. Simple, my accent was from another canton!

Some years ago, we rented an apartment in a beautiful farmhouse in a village with four houses, six families and two herds of cows. Across the road, no problem. A big, scruffy farm with a huge dungheap and a crazy cock on top; a farmer and his wife with four or five grown-up offspring, all built in a way that would make a brick convenience look rather frail. Generous and kindly folk, they loved our kids, who would come home with a nice aroma of cow manure and a freshly baked piece of apple cake in their grubby hands. Jeannot, the eldest of the farmer' sons, took the herd up to an alp in the Jura every summer. Not a loquacious man, he was more at ease with his beasts than with us boring chattering bipeds.

Next door to us, a virtuous retired sawmill worker was quite another kettle of fish. His wife was almost always out of sight—the clatter of pots by the kitchen window or thick ankles under a flutter of washing down by the pear trees. We only ever met him when he had a complaint. For example I'd be pushing the lawnmower across the last strip of our acre or so of lawn at dusk and he'd call me over to the gap in the fence.

"Monsieur, bonsoir," he would greet me. "Council regulations forbid you to use the lawnmower after 1900 hours."

I would thank him profusely. One must live inside the law.

Mind you, there are odd folk everywhere in this country. I've heard stories of people who weren't allowed to take a bath after ten at night for fear of waking the nice man next door through the wall, or of a sick old bastard who actually shot some kids with his service pistol for talking too loudly, one summer evening, five floors down on the street.

Get Integrated

As everywhere the best way to get integrated is to be of some use. One year there was nearly a metre of snow and it happened that our car was the only one that could whack and drift its way along the road, visible by bean poles planted on either side at intervals. We went out and got bread for everyone. Or maybe I was the only one damn fool enough to have a go at driving. Anyway it gave us some kind of profile, and even neighbour woodman accepted his loaf—and scrupulously paid me the price to the last centime.

On Cows

Australians have their kangaroo, the English the bulldog and the Chinese their dragon, but the Swiss have an eminently practical and affectionate beast as their emblem: the cow. Indeed Switzerland is the only country apart from India where the cow is sacred.

Alp descent in the Bern uplands.

Foreign folk occasionally set up house in picturesque Swiss villages and then complain about the noise of cowbells outside their windows early in the morning. This is a major diplomatic mistake. Cowbells and large blowflies from next door's stable crawling over your windowpanes, which rattle as tractors tow expensive subsidised machinery past your door at 5 am, are part of the charm of country life here as elsewhere in Europe.

Cows go back rather a long way in this country, some three thousand years at least. While the Egyptians were piling up their pyramids, little hairy Helvetians watched their big grey beasts grazing on their swamps and plateaus, and patiently milked them and nurtured them as an invaluable source of food and warmth.

Their enormous reputation grew, above all in the 18th century when different Swiss cheeses became export items and sources of national pride and revenue, much as had happened in Holland a century earlier. Most of Switzerland's most beautiful farms date from the late-17th to the mid-19th century and reflect this prosperity based on hard work, a wonderful demonstration of the virtues of good husbandry, early rising and hard slog.

Three kinds of cows are found in Switzerland. The classic Brown Swiss is a heavy beast that weighs in at three-quarter tonnes and can produce five tonnes of milk in a good year. The aesthetically pleasing one that gets onto postcards is the marginally smaller Simmental—a lovely golden-brown beast ornamented with white spots. The third is the black Herens cow, with horns shaped like an RAF moustache and often with a neat roll of brown hair between them. This breed only grows to about half a tonne, but is a fighting-fit, high-altitude beast.

Cow Tales

There is even bovine literature, with authors like Jeremias Gotthelf (a singularly appropriate penname for Albert Bizius, 1797–1854), a Bernois clergyman writer, who leaves us with a wonderful document of the hardships and life of the farmers, rich and poor, in the Emmental region. Nowadays, you can find an Internet site and a magazine column signed by a truculent black cow, Boubou, in the *Vachmag*, who is not overly flattering about us miserable and rather bossy bipeds.

There is an annual ritual when the Herens cows go back onto their mountain and lock horns to establish who is to be the leader of the herd for the year. (The animal's production could actually be higher, but they are bred primarily for their combativeness.) During this fight, the owners—tough Valais mountain peasants—enthusiastically feast and place bets on their champions over a glass of their slightly treacly and very heady white wine.

Although Swiss cows are as a rule as gentle as their counterparts elsewhere in the world, there are a few rules I would ask you to respect, dear reader, as much to avoid upsetting the susceptibilities of these gentle beasts as to avoid injury from them or possibly their owners.

As you wander around this lovely land you will often be in fields with cows, fenced in by an electric fence, or simply trooping free in a carefully organised space out in the wilds.

Obviously the first and foremost rule is 'Keep gates as found'. If a gate or hotwire is open there is surely a reason.

Second rule: 'Never get between a cow and her calf'. Calves are beautiful doe-like little creatures, not at all shy and irresistibly charming. But even the mildest cow will turn into a ferocious beast and charge you if she catches you messing about with junior. Put yourself in her place.

Third rule is show affection and tolerance to these ancient and very curious beasts. If you stand still, or sit down in a shady spot in their field they will come and say hello, usually in a large respectful circle. They will want to have a good look at you, perhaps sniff you a bit and then see what entertainment you can offer them. Your picnic will not interest them; your shock of red hair or your fancy sunhat, all white with little Swiss flags on it, might. They will not eat you; they are very definitely herbivores. If you talk to them, perhaps scratch them a little on their face (which they cannot reach with any of their many appendages and protuberances), they will be pleased, and eventually go about their business again.

Last rule is 'Keep clear of bulls'. Much more rarely found in pastures, bulls are instantly recognisable by various features of their bovine anatomy. They do not, generally, have the gentle characteristics of their wives and are liable to interpret any intrusion as potential rivalry to their polygamous bliss. So watch your step, avoid getting between the bull and his herd, and keep up a business-like trek along the trail, which he will recognise as leading *through* the field rather than trying to invade it. And keep some kind of escape route in mind: the nearest fence, the nearest stream or some kind of impassable barrier.

Only a fool or a matador would provoke a bull deliberately. Make sure your children know this.

Another Cow Tale

At the height of the BSE (Bovine Spongiform Encephalopathy) or Mad Cow scare, I was zapping through the satellite channels on the television late one night. I was suddenly in an Indian village where a turbaned Sikh was sitting under a big tree surrounded by beautiful bovines. "Cows eating cows, It's not right" he was saying as the gentle ruminants nodded in agreement. "Cows eat grass". Yes indeed.

SWISS SOCIETY

CHAPTER 4

"Inside the Museums infinity goes up on trial."
—Bob Dylan

PERCEPTIONS

Most people think of chocolate and watches when they think of Switzerland and, indeed, apart from the mountains, these are probably Switzerland's best-known products and a considerable source of revenue and employment.

Chocolate

Historically, cocoa beans started being imported into Europe in the 18th century. Chocolate houses sprang up, where the beans were laboriously ground into a paste and thence made into a drink with milk and sugar.

This fashion of preparing the drink, which ascribed (rightly!—I speak as a certified addict) innumerable medical, narcotic and aphrodisiacal properties to the humble cocoa plant, coincided with what has become known as the Age of Enlightenment culminating in the Industrial Revolution. Many important discussions between men of wit, science and industry would have taken place over steaming cups of chocolate. I draw a chaste curtain over boudoir scenes with crinolined and stayed ladies and their powdered beaux and leave the reader in the salacious company of Restif de la Bretonne, Rowlandson, Fragonard and their peers. No wonder the city of Zürich prohibited chocolate in 1722 because of its alleged effects on lasciviousness.

The Magic of Chocolate Head

It happened on the last day of a three-day workshop on printing at the art school where I was working—a flurry of students frantically scrambling for the presses, the invited tutor from Bordeaux surrounded by a knot of people waving paper at him. Tempers are on a short leash, no one has slept enough. Then Niklaus, the assistant—a resourceful, bright lad from Basel, walks in with a huge bar of chocolate, and announces the heavenly substance in a lilting Swiss-German accent, neatly unwrapping and breaking the bar up into squares. Nimble fingers grab their share, a silence ensues and, well, a few prints might have a very slight brown staining somewhere on the edge, but the magic has worked—a new energy grips us all, the Macintosh screens shine brighter, the cutter has a new edge, the jam of the laser printer is alleviated, the world is a better place. Chocolate, the benign and utterly legal drug, has done its bit to make life pleasant.

What distinguished Switzerland in the first decades of the 19th century was the industrial manufacture of the cocoa paste—using water-powered mills for the long grind—and its incorporation into milk to make the first basic milk chocolate.

The names Suchard (in the Neuchâtel region) and Lindt (in the Zürich region) are associated with this elaboration, and both are still major manufacturers of very fine chocolate today. Remember, we're looking at an industrial food-making process in a country where everything falls into place in the toy box. Swiss chocolate is almost invariably delicious, seems to be a brisk source of revenue nationally and is consumed with great enthusiasm by the Swiss—who hold some kind of world record for delicately nibbling or occasionally gobbling up the stuff.

Record Nibbles

Can you imagine that the resident population of Switzerland—from bawling babe to centenarian nodding in his armchair—puts away 11.6 kg of chocolate per person per year? Nor could I, until a quick calculation of my own daily chocolate intake led me to a figure of over 12 kg a year!

Don't tell the Swiss this, but the French, Dutch, Belgians, even Germans and Brits make very fine chocolate too. Few of their brands, however, have quite the international resonance of Cailler, Lindt or Nestlé. The last has become a pretty aggressive multinational conglomerate, buying up other smaller chocolate manufacturers in the market.

At the other end of the scale, as you wander about in Swiss towns and cities, you will come across many a chocolaterie which will have its own inhouse chocolates, delicious cream pralines and cakes on display. Indulge, enjoy and, above all, buy them for friends. A box of chocolates never goes amiss here—a little present when visiting someone, or coupled with a bunch of flowers pinched from a city park when patching up with a lady friend, and of course, they're wonders to take with you when you visit your cousins in Cape Town or Calgary. A word of caution: travel by air, and stay in air-conditioned spaces with them. And you might like to keep them separate from valuable items, otherwise, you might end up like me. I once packed my Leica camera and some wonderful milk chocolate together in a rucksack for a mountain walk on a hot day. Messy...

Turned Tables

Once, when a group of us were on a French-Swiss mission to Egypt, we were confronted with an ultimate culture-shock situation. A local archaeologist gave us a box of Egyptian chocolates as a present. They must have cost him a packet, and he expected us to eat them with joy and pleasure. Sadly, to a palate so accustomed to the refined taste of Swiss chocolate, these were a shade worse than English chocolates of a few decades ago. Remember the ones with jelly or salted prune fillings? Nonetheless, we made the best of the situation and offered our thanks.

If you want to mail chocolate to friends, it is better to send blocks than more fancy stuff, and definitely by airmail or some other form of rapid courier. It'll cost you more than the chocolate, but there's little point your loved ones receiving grey, disfigured muck that sticks to its wrapping.

Watches: What Makes Them Tick?

The earlier suggestion with chocolates does not apply to Swiss watches, where, even in secure registered mail, the postage cost will represent but a few per cent of the merchandise

expedited. There are cheap watches available in Switzerland, of course, the best known being the legendary Swatch; but at the upper end, the sky is the limit and some people would mortgage their mothers-in-law for a Rolex, Patek-Phillipe or Vacheron Constantin.

Again, the name of the game is production and marketing. A lot of fine watchmakers of the Huguenot faith arrived in Switzerland as refugees from France after the revocation of

Admiring the timepieces on display at the Vacheron Constantin boutique; the brand is one of the jewels of the Swiss watchmaking industry.

the Edict of Nantes (1692). They brought with them their know-how and a good Protestant industriousness, and settled predominantly in Geneva and the Jura region. It was, in many ways, the ideal industry for a country where labour is rather expensive, where there are few raw materials available and which has an excellent technical infrastructure. You can set up a watch factory in a village where land prices are not too high, and where you can profit from the cottage-industry tradition on which watchmaking was built in the 18th and 19th century. But the Swiss watch industry really came into its own in the 20th century, when Swiss precision engineering in general became a legend, nurtured by the fact that Switzerland managed to wriggle out of Europe's traumatic conflicts by its neutrality.

The Rolex Experience

Rolex pioneered the waterproof watch in 1926 and ran a brilliant advertising campaign featuring adventurers and explorers. Full-page advertisements showed these wearers casually reading the time in cockle-shell boats in the mid-Pacific, or in darkest Borneo surrounded by beady-eyed head-hunters, or on polar expeditions with only a faithful pack of huskies for company.

The Jura region, between Switzerland and France, has a rich tradition of its artisans battling for their rights and turning out production of exceptionally fine quality, which would later surface in Paris and elsewhere. The makers' names, initially scratched on the mechanism, were eventually neatly engraved on the enamelled face, and the pieces of certain makers became more and more sought after. Some artisans did only piecework—fine gold-plated watch hands, dials or minute gear wheels—precisely cut to the specifications of a watchmaking firm down in the valley.

Our friend's father in Solothurn—a picturesque, sleepy watchmaking town at the foot of the Jura—had a workshop in the back garden of his house with a couple of other elderly artisans in grey storeman's coats, with specs and micrometers in their pockets and magnifying glasses attached to their brow with iridescent steel bands. They produced

cogwheels with a few machine tools that looked about as old as they were: a cutter, a press, an adapted lathe and a number of sophisticated measuring instruments. Their week's production would fit into a smallish, flat chocolate box and would be taken by courier to one of the five or six nearby factories, the best known being Omega, in Bienne.

There was a major crisis in the 1970s when the watch market was flooded by digital watches—basically a circuit chip, a digital display and a flat case—which could be produced anywhere in the world for a thirtieth of the cost of even the simplest mechanical timepiece, and kept perfect time. The industry lost something like 80,000 workplaces, many of them semi-skilled factory hands; a number of the manufacturers, above all in the budget sector, went to the wall.

Two things happened. There seemed to be a demand in wealthier countries and circles for a prestige luxury item to tell the time, and makes that had imposed their brands and their reputation for excellence worldwide as fine watchmakers marketed their production intensely. Quartz-piloted and very accurate crystal watches with a small battery became fashionable especially if the brand name was known. They cost rather more than similar (and just as accurate) timepieces of Asian fabrication but many people seemed happy to pay the price. There was, and still is, a flourishing black market for fake Rolexes and other great makes, which, I am told, often work as well (at least initially) as their more expensive counterparts.

New market developments in automatic and self-winding mechanical watches with endless complications and ever-greater precision began to impose themselves as well. Small manufacturers arrive at every watch fair with new marvels of compactness, elaboration and beauty, and the big watchmakers are enjoying a boom in the last decade that is nothing short of spectacular. Their factories are glass-and-steel palaces on the edges of Geneva and other Swiss cities; the job sections of the daily papers have half-page ads looking for new staff; and the firms are pouring money into sponsorship and various forms of publicity. A photographer friend who has a contract with Rolex drives a Porsche to his spacious house in one of Geneva's more salubrious villages. I looked at a fine-watch catalogue the other day and discovered that you can pick up a limited-edition signed Vacheron Constantin for the price of my pal's Porsche. And people seem happy to do so. You can also pay ten times that price for an authentic mint-condition model from the 1920s.

Then there came a man with a concept fairly similar to the highly economical Volkswagen Beetle. A Swiss industrialist from Lebanon, Nicholas Hajek founded the Swatch enterprise. As Swiss labour costs were considered high, his solution was to get ever more elaborate machine tools that virtually had a bar of metal going in one end and a completed watch popping out the other, under the watchful eye of a Turkish or Portuguese immigrant labourer backed by a bossy Swiss in a white coat. When material costs were up, he used synthetic materials in the place of expensive alloys. A lot of money was put, however, into marketing. There were huge, huge advertising and marketing budgets, with artists commissioned to work on the concepts of new lines of watches; don't you want an original limited edition creation on your wrist?

The end result was an amazing bubble of commerce that persists to this day, a varied and ever-renewing collection of watches at the price of a good restaurant meal, no-frills but good little timekeepers that you won't bother to fix if they break down—the Nikes of the watch world. This, in turn, has also created a whole pool of employment and activity around it, and made Biel/Bienne—on the edge of the Jura, where the Swatch works are based (along with the more traditional but also superb middle-range watch Omega)—into something of a boom town.

Hayek has since launched a car with a similar high-end design concept: the Smart, produced with Mercedes-Benz in the Strasbourg region, outside Basel. Though not that cheap compared to Japanese imports, it attracts a good following from a somewhat eccentric market that used to run around in Citroën 2CVs and Volkswagen Beetles.

PLAYING SOLDIERS

Another widespread perception of Switzerland, which is only partly accurate, has to do with its army. It is true that in the 20th century Switzerland backed up its neutrality with a massive people's militia. Every male between 18 and 42 had a rifle behind the door, and was, at least in theory, ready to run out of the house with a sandwich under his arm to take pot-shots at the advancing columns of enemies. Ammunition was kept sealed in a tin resembling a beer can so that you would not be tempted to shoot your neighbour when his stereo was on too loud (as happens once in a while). All Swiss males were inducted by a recruiting office; most underwent an initial three months' training and were then called up for two weeks every year after that for further military training. Refusal to serve or to be promoted to the rank of an officer were jailable offences. For this reason, I work with a number of ex-jailbirds of my own generation who are otherwise the most pleasant and principled people I know.

Soldiers boarding a train. Swiss males are given basic training at the age of 18 and further annual sessions as the country maintains a people's militia.

Popular mythology claims that the Swiss standing army and its fortifications kept various enemy invaders at bay during the two World Wars. In fact, things are a little more complicated than that. In the 1914–1918 war, Switzerland was nominally neutral but there was a very important Germanophile movement in the country that did everything in its power to aid and abet the Kaiser's forces and supply Germany with arms and matériel. Their most important act

Troops disbanding in the court of a municipally owned castle.

was to place one of their own, the Prussian-trained Ulrich Wille, as Supreme General of the Swiss Armed Forces—a man so disgraceful during and after the conflict that there continues to be little to no information on him on the Internet. In the aftermath of the war, there was considerable tension between the French- and the German-speaking regions, exacerbated by the social problems of the time.

In World War II, the troops were led by a man of considerable integrity, the waspish Vaudois general Henri Guisan, who certainly ran into some nasty trouble with pro-Nazi elements in the Swiss administration but managed to keep the country militarily on the knife-edge of neutrality. Initially, the bulk of the army retreated to fortresses in the Swiss Alps, leaving a skeleton force in the plains; bridges and other infrastructure were mined with explosive charges.

But, as Paul Bilton in his book *The Xenophobe's Guide to the Swiss* laconically states, 'The truth is that no power-crazed dictator is going to attack the country where he's stashed away his millions'.

More serious writers like Max Frisch wrote about the fabulous business the Swiss did with the belligerent powers, above all, with the Axis side—which was closer to hand then England or the US. It is also known that firms such as Ford Motors (whose boss was a notorious anti-Semite) continued business in wartime Germany through Swiss intermediaries—which probably also left a few dollars in Swiss bankers' hands.

As part of the Cold War paranoia after World War II, each Swiss house was supposed to have a nuclear-proof bomb shelter. Swiss hausfraus were also legally obliged to keep a supply of staple foods, water and toilet paper there for stays of up to three weeks. The scheme added considerably to building prices, and kept some enterprises who were in the business of supplying heavy concrete doors and other fancy stuff nice and fat. Then around the time the Berlin Wall fell, Swiss people began to realise that they would never lock their families and themselves into a bunker to later emerge into a nuclear winter. The scheme has been quietly dropped for all practical purposes.

Other vestiges include the odd mountain fortress, often camouflaged as part of cliffs, that leads into labyrinthine tunnel complexes of the Maginot variety. The government has started to flog off these installations as surplus. Their maintenance and staffing costs must have been colossal. One fortress is now a hotel; others have become cute and rather odd holiday homes, usually with spectacular views. Many of the wine-growers around here clatter around in a bewildering variety of army surplus four-wheel-drives. And the Georgian keeper of an 18th-century castle down the lake from us has a Centurion tank in his garden.

The Swiss army also took a close look at its military account books, and drastically reduced its manpower demands from about half a million 20 years ago to less than 200,000 today. This, at long last, facilitated the position of conscientious objectors and other refuseniks. Switzerland still seems to have a lot of soldiers, though; you will see them behind barbed wire in front of some of the more sensitive UN missions of belligerent states; you will see them in Kosovo as part of the UN peacekeeping force (the policy of neutrality having been quietly dropped in relation to certain UN operations, although Switzerland definitely is not about to join NATO or any such alliance). And you saw medical troops with rescue equipment after the disastrous Asian Tsunami in 2004.

The alternative to the army, now available to all young males in Switzerland who will go to the trouble to build up a case, is a 24-month *civil* national service, where the person works in some organisation dedicated to the improvement of the human or environmental condition. They are given a modest salary and housed at the site where they are working, if necessary. So our eldest son spent eight months building stone walls at various mountain sites. This was a very happy choice for him: he adores mountains and the open air, and he met a lot of people from other parts of the country, made an effort to learn their languages and to see what made them tick. Subsequently he worked for a Protestant charity, driving a van about picking up second-hand furniture. He is hoping to do some overseas aid next, after he's completed his studies.

Nevertheless the army still represents an enormous slice of the Swiss national budget, and is obviously a good testing ground for Switzerland's small but vigorous arms industry to sell their wares.

Jokes to the contrary notwithstanding, the Swiss do not have a navy. I did once, however, see a company of soldiers drifting down the Rhône in rubber dinghies on a foggy morning, bobbing in the direction of France, waving their paddles and their assault rifles. They seemed cheerful and chattered away in Swiss-German without seeming to have too clear a notion of where they were and where they were heading. The French, one supposes, handled this invasion attempt with their usual devastating efficiency. We never heard of them again. I suppose they have been interned in

Guyana or inducted into the French foreign legion by now, part of a long tradition of Swiss mercenaries serving foreign princes.

My Life as a Soldier

As a Swiss citizen, I was eventually snaffled up and drafted into the army as an auxiliary (unarmed!) soldier in the instruction section at the federal military headquarters in Bern. Life was pretty easy actually, and I was called up usually for a fortnight every two years. I clumped about in my inelegant field-grey uniform and indestructible boots, working mainly in the beautifully appointed studios and darkrooms of the film photo section, eating in the federal military department's cafeteria and sleeping in Victorian barracks in an austere and somewhat draughty 48-bed room where I rigged up a discreet extension cord for a little reading lamp

Now one calm morning, as I was hanging out films to dry, the big, black military telephone rang.

"Hello, Herr Oettli," simpered a Swiss-German voice. "Here is Fräulein Blitzli."

"Yes Fräulein, very nice. What can I do for you on this auspicious April morning?"

"Herr Oettli, I am Colonel Chröpfli's personal assistant."

"Yes, yes, very pleased I'm sure. Um?"

"Now, Herr Oettli, this morning during the coffee break, Colonel Chröpfli saw you in the cafeteria with two other auxiliary soldiers."

Possible, the place is packed full of athletic-looking middle-aged men in polyester suits, who are mostly high-ranking military personnel. We soldiers are under orders to salute only officers wearing their kepis—not all that easy when you're carrying a tray, but officers usually have the decency to leave their headgear off indoors.

"Y-yes I was there; go there every day at 8:50 am and leave at 9:05 am."

"And Herr Oettli, the colonel noticed that your shirt was unbuttoned at the top and your tie was loosened. Now, at your workplace, you are entitled to arrange your clothes to ease your work if authorised by your NCO, but in the cafeteria, we must insist that a certain discipline in regards to your appearance is necessary. The military regulations are very explicit about this and loose ties or unbuttoned shirts and so on are not authorised. I hope you understand, Herr Oettli, and that you will conform to the rule in future."

"Fräulein Blitzli, I am completely crestfallen and utterly apologetic about this inexcusable oversight. Rest assured that from this day on, I shall present myself as a spick and span example of the finest in Swiss military sartorial splendour. Thank you again, Fräulein, for pointing this out to me and please rest assured of my eternal and patriotic devotion..." etc.

Continued on next page

Continued from previous page

Then I do a small double take. Obviously the suited man who saw my transgression did not consider a brief personal remark appropriate in the relatively congenial atmosphere of the cafeteria. Instead, he would have looked at the regimental number on the shoulder pads of my military shirt, would have got Fräulein Blitzli to check at security which auxiliary soldiers from the Geneva regiment were working at the military department that day, would have inspected the identity photographs, and would have got the Fräulein to track me down like a fox in his lair. The total operation would have tied the two of them up for at least an hour.

A small incident which gave me an understanding of military logic as applied in the small and very polite world of Switzerland.

VIRTUE AND VICE

As an ex-Calvinist there are a number of aspects of life which I can most conveniently treat under this heading. We are all faced with endless moral choices, and the angel and the devil in our souls combat valiantly to turn us one way or the other. To some extent, the country we live in will give us a framework to act on at least some of our higher and baser desires.

Vice

Let's start with vice. We are all of us in the grip of one or another of its manifestations; a totally virtuous life would be as boring as a totally vice-ridden one would be wasted. But I am leaving the path of the simple guide and becoming a bit too moral philosophic. If you need moral guidance, there are other books for that.

Smoking

So, let us start with that widespread and health-threatening vice, smoking. Switzerland is pretty tolerant, and tobacco products are also cheaper here than in most of the surrounding countries. I won't go into any cause-and-effect reasoning, but many of the larger English and American cigarette makers have important manufacturing, administrative or research centres here. Cigars are locally available, ranging from the very worst known (Villiger and Rössli) to some of the finest, of which Davidoff, a Russian brand based in Geneva, is the international reference. There are local variants: in the Tessin region an evil twisty cheroot is produced in Brissago with which my father used to stink out his study. In the picturesque Appenzell region, farmers smoke what smell like goats' droppings in tiny little pipes with exquisitely tooled silver lids.

Switzerland has a federal law against passive smoking indoors, which effectively forces people to smoke outside.

The law on smoking has undergone changes here as it has elsewhere. The Federal Council accepted that passive smoke could be regarded as a health hazard, and smoking is hence banned inside most buildings; all smoking compartments and areas in public transport have also been eliminated (not sure about the upper decks on lake steamers).

The situation in bars and restaurants was left to the cantons to regulate, and as I write there is quite a patchwork. In general there is provision made in most cantons to have a smoking zone in establishments above a certain size. Tessin, for example, follows the Italian model of having a covered 'open-air' area attached to its cosy cafés; others are more draconian. Best to find out by looking around wherever you are.

If you visit someone, you will quickly sense whether the household is a smoking one or not, and you could also ask if lighting up is authorised to avoid making a faux pas. If the weather is not too horrible, you could always slip out onto the balcony for a discreet light up.

In workplaces, much depends on how and where you work, as anywhere in the world. If you work for the World Health Organisation (WHO), for example, smoking at your desk would be a terrible idea. But when I go and see our smart lawyer bloke, he usually offers me a Davidoff from a glass-fronted cabinet in his sumptuous office, which I politely refuse but suspect he bills me for anyway.

Drugs

Like elsewhere in Europe, other smoking materials—less legal ones—are also available. In terms of grass, Switzerland has been remarkably tolerant, and the window boxes and rooftops of our city show a lot of enthusiastic home cultivation during the spring and early summer. The stuff is technically illegal, but the law is rarely enforced except in conjunction with other confrontations with the police. So although cantonal police forces seem to have tightened up somewhat in recent years, the long-term trend seems to be towards a continuing liberalisation. Dealing is discouraged and can lead to prosecution, especially if it involves large quantities or supplying minors. As elsewhere in more or less civilised countries, a distinction is made between a small stash for personal consumption and a suitcase full of imported BC Bud or Durban Poison. There are no Amsterdam-style coffee shops here, and attempts to launch them have generally been suppressed by the state police. Adolescents are advised at junior high school of the dangers of excessive consumption and given counselling on the facts of the whole gamut of drugs without the thing blowing into a major issue in general.

As far as the major addictive opiate and cocaine-based drugs are concerned, Switzerland has a pragmatic policy. The country was, for many years, at the centre of some pretty sordid international drug-dealing rings involving refugees, diplomats and impoverished Third World 'mules' who came into the airports as 'tourists' with a bellyful of coke or whatever muck was being imported. Eventually, the Swiss came up with an interesting solution for defusing the situation. So for the last decade, these drugs have been available free in government-funded distribution centres, where the unfortunate shivering addicts queue up for their daily supply and are given medical and social care as required.

The programme is associated with substitution therapy involving methadone and other substances. This work has attracted the interest of other European states who are finding the problem impossibly onerous and socially wasteful, to put it mildly, as it clogs their judicial system and packs their gaols and psychiatric secure units with occasional dope smokers, cringing junkies and confrontational petty dealers.

Ecstasy and other stimulants are available clandestinely in clubs and dance places, but they remain strictly prohibited and, as elsewhere in the world, you would be definitely at risk both judicially and medically if your needs run in that direction.

Gambling

Swiss residents seem to gamble quite a lot, if statistics are to be believed. And the authorities have an ambiguous attitude to this very popular and lucrative vice. In 2004, with deregulation nationally implemented—but still with a restriction in the number of casinos—gains were up a cool 37 per cent. Half of this went to the federal government for social and other spending (so perhaps gambling should be included in virtue rather than vice?).

Our smaller casinos have a rather distinguished history, with the exploits of people like Dostoyevsky in the definitely provincial setting of Saxon in the Valais. At least he allowed Prince Myshkin to saunter past there, giving rise to one of his most intriguing works, *The Idiot*. For a long time, the casinos in the country were strictly controlled with a maximum 5-franc bet. The betting limit has now been raised but nevertheless many people prefer to bet in the great establishments in neighbouring countries. I can cite at random Meersburg in Baden-Württemberg (Germany), Bregenz (Austria) in the east, and Evian and Divonne across the border in France in the Lake Geneva region. I have personally eaten very well and lost respectably in the latter.

Lotteries are popular too. A well-run national lottery, or Lotto, gives good prizes to a lucky few, and vast contributions to cultural and social foundations. There seems to be a football pool as well, run by the same foundation, although

I know little about it. There are also Europe-wide and Internet-based lotteries, with truly staggering gains as a very remote possibility. Horses and dogs have their place here as elsewhere, although they are not as popular as those races in England, Ireland and France. You can bet on horses in special pubs called PMU, with many, many people quietly watching the geegees scrambling across the television screen in the corner and watching their bets evaporate. These places are generally very smoky, as the predilection for punting and for smoking seem to co-occur.

Illegal Gambling Dens

There are also illegal gambling circles where card games are played. These may take some squirrelling out, though one occasionally comes across them by accident. There was this quiet suburban Chinese restaurant that hardly did any business as far as I could see, until the time I happened to walk past their door at two in the morning. The curtains were closed and big cars with diplomatic number plates were pulled up outside. Peeping through the curtains, I saw a circle of men around a table, mostly Asians. Some were wearing their hats, a few were wearing their coats, one actually had a green eyeshade. Pensively, I wandered on.

Drinking

Alcohol consumption is in line with most European countries, and its purchase is restricted to adults. If you're having a meal *en famille* in a restaurant, you are, naturally, entitled to let your adolescent offspring have a glass of wine, but minors would not, generally, be allowed on their own into cafés and restaurants that serve alcoholic beverages. Again, a law of common sense applies. The rather scruffy bistro across the road from our son's old college would naturally allow 17- or 18-year-olds in to drink a tea or a chocolate, or even a glass of beer on a hot afternoon. But if there were any incidents, the licensee would have to answer to the authorities and licences are easily revoked and hard to obtain. Beer and cider are available over the counter at shops and supermarkets to those 16 years and on, wine and spirits from 18.

There are drunks about in Switzerland, but rather fewer than in other Anglo-Saxon or East European countries; the frequency seems to be roughly the same as junkies, and public tolerance of them about on par.

In contrast to the Anglo-American system, café or pub opening hours are pretty liberal and it is possible to get a glass of wine or a whisky if you're strolling around in the city well after midnight. It is also possible to get a very expensive glass of wine or whisky in nightclubs. Let the drinker beware! The establishment is obliged to mark prices, but there are clip joints here as elsewhere.

Prostitution

And that brings us to the ladies of the night. Prostitution is illegal but tolerated, with rather strict police control on the sex workers and their activities. There has been, and sporadically still is, gang involvement in importing girls from poorer countries who are then put on the sex market and often subjected to ill-treatment, and there, the police and federal authorities are very vigilant.

Most ladies though, and gentlemen too, work quietly in a very private sphere as professionals. Some cities have put housing blocks at their disposal, which enables them to work with a minimum of security and social help. The staid and respectable daily papers in the main centres usually have a page or two of lurid and surprisingly varied ads catering to all imaginable tastes. Street ladies, from what I've seen of them, seem to be somewhat geriatric, or young but dangerously flaky. In the red-light districts of some cities, there is a presence of the state health and social service department, which gives out information and contraceptives to keep AIDS in check.

Virtue

One of the finer things I've seen is a soup stand offering free hot soup to the poor, manned by Geneva's prostitutes, at the flea market when the winter cold starts to pinch. If you live in a Swiss centre, you will quickly get to know the various associations that help out both locally and internationally. I'll list some of the more important charities at the end of the book, many of which are global organisations and probably already known to you.

Children in traditional costume representing the various Swiss regions gather at the parade marking the bicentenary of the Unspunnen Stone in the Interlaken area.

Trains are the main form of transportation between towns in Switzerland—a quick and easy way to get across the rolling terrain.

Switzerland's mountainous terrain is popular with trekkers. Among the 'hazards' faced are the overly-friendly cows who roam the countryside.

A skating rink in the courtyard of Basel's Museum of Art. Switzerland's geographical location and climate make it a great destination for winter sports such as ice-skating and skiing.

Traditional timber houses in the village of Grimentz in Val d'Anniviers, nestled in the Swiss Alps. Most Swiss people live in small towns and villages.

A typical Swiss dish is fondue. Cubes of bread are dipped in a warm sauce made of cheese heated over a small burner.

One of the best-known is, of course, the Red Cross. Formed by Henri Dunant in the 19th century, it monitors wars and the treatment of prisoners and victims (the famous Geneva Convention), and recruits volunteers to help with first-aid, nursing and disaster relief. The Red Cross also runs excellent used-clothes shops. So do some charities, notably the Salvation Army and the Catholic and Protestant social services, who also collect and sell used furniture and books.

Naturally, if you are religious, there is a whole network of churches, parishes, mosques and synagogues of all tendencies. In Geneva, for example, there are at least seven English-language parishes, and two German-language ones, as well as those using Italian, Spanish and Portuguese, often covering everything from high Catholicism to Presbyterianism and other odder sects as well.

Mormons wander about with their white shirts and their labels earnestly trying to convert us all. Meanwhile saffron-clad Buddhist monks and big-hatted, bearded Jews catch the number 12 tram. The Greeks have their church, the Russians have a beautiful little basilica in the traditional style, and the Romanians have just built a lovely wooden church in the suburbs. I know of three well-attended synagogues, each with a traditional or more progressive tendency, and there is a splendid mosque for an active and committed Muslim population.

Nationally the two major religions, though, are Roman Catholicism (now in the majority) and Protestantism. The latter has a strong non-hierarchical and Presbyterian tendency based on the teachings of Ulrich Zwingli in the Swiss-German areas and John Calvin in Geneva, both partly inspired by Martin Luther, the German reformer, and by the humanism of Erasmus.

In Geneva, Calvin and his follower Théodore de Bèze had strong theocratic tendencies and the city state was a pretty joyless and repressive place. In 1685, Louis XV, under pressure, revoked the Edict of Nantes—which had guaranteed religious tolerance in that country—and many

Huguenot refugees arrived in Geneva. Solid citizens and hard workers, they also had rather more progressive ideas than the local Ayatollahs and made the place a little more reasonable and liberal. Historically, most of Switzerland's cantons were originally considered Catholic or Protestant, and a good deal of religious warring marred the 16th and early 17th century here. The area east of the lake of Bienne is a patchwork of enclaves with Protestant villages flying the Vaud flag, juxtaposed with Catholic enclaves attached to Fribourg. There are also strong associative secular tendencies, above all in the anarchist socialist workers' movements in the Jura, and in a strong anti-clerical tendency among many older Swiss-Italians whose ancestors often arrived here to escape religious persecution in Italy.

Religious tolerance and secular institutions have been guaranteed constitutionally since 1848. In similar circumstances to Jules Ferry's in France, the Jesuits were sent packing when, in the spirit of Pius IX's reactionary positions, they attempted (or were suspected of attempting) to interfere with the secular state and its education in 1873. They were not allowed on Swiss ground again until a century later. In the interim, an independent Catholic movement which did not recognise the authority of Rome was founded in Basel and Geneva in the 1880s. It is still in existence today.

The Cost of Religion

The financing of religion in this country is based on a voluntary religious tax which you can fill out on your tax form, carefully defining the denomination to which you would like your taxes forwarded. This allows you also to pay nothing to any religious organisation if you so prefer.

TROUBLE IN TOYLAND

The Swiss police, like the American one, is organised on a state level. Each canton has its own uniform, and occasionally, there are slight differences in practice or attitudes to the job. These usually reflect the mores of the canton. Ferociously armed, the police are not generally as trigger-happy as their transatlantic counterparts. Apart from the occasional scandal inevitable in any democracy, the police here are known to be reasonably competent and correct in most circumstances. Naturally, a lot depends from which side you meet them—as a respectable resident lodging a complaint or as a participant in some offence or legal problem.

Let's tackle the first category. We might find our home burgled, our car with a window smashed in a car park, or some assault or other affair involving our sons or daughters late at night. Switzerland is not immune to any of these nasty incidents and there should never be a reason to hesitate to call in the police. They will be on the scene quite rapidly and provide the assistance required in criminal investigations and the organisation of such help as you may need in the first instance. I would stress, however, that on your part you must come clean with them as well. If your own papers in relation to Swiss residency are not in order, if your car is not registered in your name or if you're trying to cook up some insurance fraud or other, the situation could backfire severely.

On the other hand, if you're at the receiving end of the long arm of the law, you will naturally have to keep your cool and make decisions regarding your own responsibility with a reasonably clear head. The likeliest thing would probably be a driving offence. Federal law is strictly enforced, if somewhat sporadically, and speeding can be quite an expensive matter. If you are driving more than 30 km (18.6 miles) over the legal limit, you are liable to be imprisoned in some cantons. The ritual alcohol and drug test can also lead to serious consequences. Again, in common with other European countries, any attempt to bribe a police officer would lead to very severe sanctions indeed and could well culminate with you sitting in one of Switzerland's comfortable but decidedly secure prisons for a while.

The Swiss have a legal tradition which is endearingly old-fashioned, based on a rather crude interpretation over

two centuries of the old French Napoleonic code, which sees an arrested person as guilty until proven innocent. A change to a more libertarian law code came into force three or four decades ago—involving *habeas corpus* and other newfangled ideas—but some policemen still find this rather hard to follow.

To complicate matters, at ministerial level, Switzerland still groups justice and police in one portfolio, leading occasionally to consequences that would raise eyebrows in magistrate courts in other European countries. What this really means is that if you think you have been unjustly treated, you'll have to fight for your rights, and the odds will be stacked against you. For minor offences carrying a mandatory fine, any opposition usually carries fees which are higher than the fine imposed, so you have to be pretty determined and on pretty solid ground to fight back. Lawyers are rather expensive (as everywhere in the world), but in most cities, there are legal centres that will give you preliminary advice for a nominal fee. Don't hesitate to use this service, including for civil questions. I have invariably found them to be useful and sound and they can occasionally sort out a minor or more important hitch with a few phone calls or a three-line letter to the right address to clarify your position. You will find them in the phone-book of the place where you live.

Peter's Tangle with the Law

My brother Peter came to live in Switzerland some years ago and went through an experience which clearly demonstrates the Swiss' highly developed sense of order—or meddlesome persistence, depending how you see it.

Peter was living in one of the quieter, more picturesque regions in the north-east and one Sunday, he and his wife set out in their little car to explore the beauty of the region. Along the way, they pulled up into a roadsiding beside a forest, and my brother saw some stones in the grass, neatly arranged to make a fire. Ex-Boy Scout that he was, he gathered some wood, rubbed two sticks together and soon, the two of them had a little blaze crackling and sausages frying on hazelnut sticks. (Incidentally, Swiss sausages, especially cervelas and Bratwurst, are delicious grilled like that, and you traditionally cut a little cross in each end which makes them open up like starfish. In this form, Swiss Germans refer to them as 'frogs'.)

The picnic over, they carefully put out the fire and strolled off for a little walk in the forest, arm in arm as befits a young couple on a Swiss-German Sunday excursion.

Imagine their surprise when, some days later, they received in their mail notification of a fine for lighting a fire in an unauthorised place. Peter went to the local police station with his bit of paper and politely asked to see the duty officer, who, equally politely, told him to pay the fine and not argue. He had apparently been denounced by a good citizen driving by in his or her car.

Peter argued that there was no sign prohibiting the lighting of fires, that there was a provision for fires in the stone fireplace on the ground, and that he had taken special care to put out the fire before leaving, scouts' honour. The man of law replied that any objection to the fine would entail paying a charge two times higher and that Peter would lose the case anyway, having been in contravention of the 1921 bylaw 44 paragraph 7 line 2b prohibiting the lighting of fires within a distance of less than 66 metres (216 feet) of a forest in the months of April to October.

Continued on next page

Leabharlanna Poiblí Chathair Bhaile Átha Cliath
Dublin City Public Libraries

Continued from previous page

Peter, one of the literate members of our family, wrote a polite but firm letter to the authorities pointing out that the interdiction was in no way signalled in the place and that in the first ten days of the month of April, a certain indulgence to a serious citizen might be considered, etc. The exchange went on for two more letters until the uniformed gentlemen, finally tired out and worn down by the weight of paper and obviously unwilling to bother an overworked magistrate, relented and let my brother off, against the payment of the by now substantial charges. Peter paid his administrative charge and felt like a decent free Swiss citizen should when his basic rights have been vindicated.

A COMEDY OF MANNERS

The residents of Switzerland are, on the whole, pretty urbane and polite, and if you do something that is out of line, they'll usually find ways of discreetly letting you know with no skin off your nose. Of course, you will find yobs and louts here too, as anywhere, but on the whole, you should be comfortable socialising.

Hello and Goodbye

The Swiss, especially the Swiss-Germans, are great at greetings and farewells. If you walk into a bakery or a shoe shop, or approach the checkout lady in the Migros supermarket, a quick hello is appreciated. When walking out of any shop empty-handed, manifest yourself in some polite way—a 'Goodbye and thank you' or a friendly wave; sneaking off is not appreciated from someone else's space.

If you meet someone in a business or social context, a firm handshake with eye contact is in order. You would use the formal address form (*Sie* in German, *vous* in French) unless you meet the person quite frequently. I have been drinking my morning coffee in the same café for two decades, and the lady and I have been on first-name terms for a good 15 years. With the baker, the pharmacist and the dentist, however, after a good decade, it's still the formal address form—which doesn't however stop us bantering or chatting happily when the occasion presents itself.

Colleagues at my workplace are strictly on first-name terms. The last director I used *vous* with; the present one is a colleague I've worked with for 20 years, and it would be foolish to revert to a more formal form of address. In the army, officers are always addressed in the formal form, and it would be wise not to address a policeman writing you a speeding ticket as *du* or *tu*. If a policeman addresses you in the intimate form, he's grilling you for a crime you've committed, and he's out of order.

It would be difficult to imagine sitting down for a meal at someone's place or even at a restaurant and keeping up the formal form of address, unless there is an important guest present, in which case the drift of the evening will remain perfectly cordial but a little more distant.

Do you dress for these occasions? Generally yes, one should at least be conscious that the occasion demands an ironed shirt for the gentlemen. Ladies, quite naturally, present themselves well here as elsewhere in the world. It would not generally be acceptable for gentlemen to turn up in shorts on a warm summer evening unless it is to the home of someone who knows you well already. Shorts have associations with holiday here, and are not even in sight in more swank workplaces.

> Take the semi-formal municipal council affair the other day (a primary school prize-giving!). A respected councillor was looked at with much askance by the mayor when the former turned up in very charming bermudas and yellow socks. The mayor, who is also the village miller and a bit of a yob, runs about in khaki shorts and singlets as he works, but when he's officiating, it's the old grey suit every time.

After a pleasant evening at someone's home, it would probably be normal for you, regardless of gender, to kiss the ladies and for the ladies to kiss one another, lightly on the cheek. Some men kiss each other too; just feel your way and see how it goes.

At the workplace, kisses are perfectly in order after an absence if there is a genuine pleasure at meeting the person again. It's a ritual at New Year's. Between men, a brisk handshake or a slap on the shoulder between colleagues does nicely too. In some places in the German part, there is a formal ritual of handshaking all round at the beginning and end of the day, but in the French part, people would find that rather tiring and makes the whole business a bit like a prize-fight.

Baptism, Birthdays, Weddings and Funerals

To be honest, I have never been invited to a baptism, as it is not a very common event in the circles we move in, but I assume that the ritual in church and the subsequent feast would take the form it does in most other Christian communities in the world. If we go and see someone who's had a baby, we'll obviously turn up with a wee gift such as a soft toy (lovely soft toys are available here!) and with lots of clucky advice. We would instinctively not make our visit too long or too intrusive.

Birthdays come in two varieties, for the young and for the older. If your child is invited to a schoolmate's birthday party, which will usually be in the early afternoon or evening, that's great. If you can make yourself available, offer to help —a gaggle of kids can be hard to handle, and it's a nice way to get to know other parents.

Presents are much as elsewhere, something small and amusing; don't go overboard. Birthday cakes, too, are like elsewhere, and the song seems to be 'Happy Birthday', occasionally translated into the local vernacular.

Big people have birthday parties too. A friend born on 29 February throws a party every four years; and she's just had her 10th birthday! For young people, there are usually bigger occasions for their 18th birthday (legal majority) and often for their 20th as well. There are often common projects at those occasions where a number of people can pitch in for something a little special.

Pizza Bash

Adults often have parties to mark decades, like the 50th birthday bash I was invited to. It turned out to be a pizza fest with the eldest son and tiny nephews briskly working on a production line inside a tent, with about 60 guests. Again, don't turn up empty handed, and don't go overboard.

Weddings tend to be pretty big occasions here, at least the first time round; usually a church ceremony of some kind followed by drinks for the masses invited. This is often followed by a dinner and dance in some appropriately chosen locality. Dress a little frilly and fancy. Formal would be indicated; morning suits and such are rare in my circles. Gifts

Special Events
Special occasions like Bar Mitzvahs and circumcisions are strictly extraterritorial, and you would know how to handle them if invited. If unsure, check with a friend in the group.

are quite varied. Often the couple will have a marriage list in some classy department store where you can sign for the footstool or the life-sized porcelain leopard depending on your means. There are usually speeches, satirical shows put on by the groom's and bride's mates, and much dancing and carousing.

I draw a discreet curtain over the stag and hen parties before a respectable nuptial. I do remember, though, one case of a demure young lady who had to dress up as a novice nun and wander around the flea market asking men to kiss her to let her have a last taste of the earthly joys before taking holy orders.

Homosexual relationships

Homosexual relationships are perfectly legal in Switzerland between consenting adults, and the gay scene runs the gamut from cruising to stable relationships. No particular stigma is attached to this sexual preference, and we have known a number of high-ranking cabinet and government ministers who were more or less discreetly homosexual.

A form of partnership allowing inheritance and access has been on the Genevan law books since 2001, for couples—hetero- or homosexual—who wish to share their lives in a formalised way based on mutual trust. The law is being extended slowly. There is still no allowance for assisted procreation.

Funerals are generally rather less fun. If the deceased was close to you, you'll probably find yourself involved in the preparations. These vary quite a bit. In Geneva, for example, the most important funeral director is a municipal service, which works at reasonable charges in a very correct and decent way. Of course, there are private morticians as well, and choices can be made. If a person dies in a hospital, you can be advised there on the various options.

Memorial or funeral services can take place in parish churches of different denominations and also in mosques and synagogues. Cemeteries and crematoriums, too, are municipal and different arrangements can be made if your religion requires them. Most of the bigger cities have Jewish cemeteries; some, like Geneva, have Muslim ones as well.

If an acquaintance, the parent of a friend or of a work colleague has died, it would be best to check the death notice in the newspaper. Most funerals are open but some are restricted to close family members. If you go, you obviously dress down a little—something dark and a little respectful is in order. Don't overdo it though: the only men wearing black suits will be the chaps from the city funeral service, and black shawls are usually the widow's lot. Flowers are usually appreciated, although sometimes the wish is for a donation to a charity of the deceased's or the family's choice. You will quickly find out whether you are also expected to go to the cemetery. I have only done this on two occasions in the 30 years here, once to the cemetery for the wife of a colleague and once to the crematorium for the son of a friend.

As I said at the start of this chapter, though, almost all of the customs and manners described are essentially based on good sense and respect. Listen and watch, go along with what people do unless you're definitely uncomfortable with it, and you'll do fine. Resist any impulse to shoot your mouth off. If you walk into a discussion of local politics and some federal councillor is being pulled apart for incompetence or stupidity, you'd be on pretty thin ground to shout agreement as a non-Swiss and a non-voter. By all means, get involved, but give it time, give it time!

WELCOME ON BOARD

CHAPTER 5

"I pity the poor immigrant."
—Bob Dylan

PAPERING IT OVER

If you plan to come to Switzerland as a medium- or long-term resident, whether for work or studies, you will have to get in touch with the consulate in your country of residence to make preliminary contact. In common with most European countries, Switzerland is not particularly welcoming to foreigners in general and you will have to make your case with some care.

Residency Permits

The authority for residency permits, applying a very tight federal law, is the canton, so you'll be dealing with the canton authorities of where you intend to stay.

Schengen Agreement

Signed by 26 countries, most of whom are part of the European Union, the Schengen Agreement provides for standard immigration policies to be implemented by all participating countries. This means that when the citizens of these countries travel to other countries which have also signed the agreement, they will be not be subjected to checks at the borders. At the same time, the agreement also enforces external border controls against anyone who isn't from a participating country. The agreement was initially signed by five countries in 1985 near the small Luxembourg town of Schengen (hence the name). Switzerland joined only in 2004 and the membership was ratified by referendum in 2005.

European Passport (EC or EFTA) Holder

As the 'outsider' in Europe, tied to the union only through the Schengen agreements, Switzerland's position is rather different from that of the countries surrounding it in this respect. If, at least on paper, the free movement of European citizens through Switzerland is authorised (the Agreement of Free Movement of Persons is recent and not too well understood), their right to be residents and to work here is still subject to a quota regimentation.

As of now, there seem to be three possibilities:

- **Short-term Residency, also called L Permits (Kurzaufenthaltsbewilligung or Séjour de courte durée)**
  These are issued, on application, to people who have arranged (from outside the borders) for a short-term work contract (less than 12 months) or to come and live here temporarily as non-earning residents, e.g. students, pensioners. In all cases, you must have proof of having sufficient financial means to provide for your own and your family's needs. You must also have health and accident insurance coverage, which, in Switzerland, is scandalously expensive.

  European nationals are allowed to enter Switzerland to look for a job and will be given a grace period of four months. During this time, you would still be considered a foreign resident. If you do find a job and hold it for at least three months, you employer will have to apply for a residency permit for you.

  Regardless of which scenario applies to you, your employer will have to make residency applications for you at the cantonal authorities and your permit will last for the duration of your employment contract. Your residency permit can be renewed by presenting your new work contract and the application can be done from within the country. Your employer should be well-versed on what to do.

  Trainee permits may be issued to people aged 18–30 who enter the country in order to improve their linguistic abilities or engage in occupational training. This permit, valid for a maximum of 18 months, comes under the purview of trainee agreements and not the Agreement of Free Movement of Persons.

Students (on the Erasmus programme or otherwise) have to show proof of enrolment and matriculation. Pensioners need to show that they are financially independent and able to support themselves. All short-term residency permits allow you to bring your family into Switzerland for the duration of your stay.

- **Residency Permit, also called B Permit**
  If you have a work contract that lasts a year or longer, you will be entitled to apply for this permit, which allows you to stay in the country for five years. If, after the five-year period, you are unemployed, you will only be allowed to renew this permit for another year. On the other hand, if you are still employed by the same company or have found some other means of supporting yourself financially, the permit can be renewed for another five years. Keep in mind that in the event you have switched jobs or moved cantons, the authorities must be notified. If you are gainfully employed, you also have the option of converting your B Permit to a Residency Permit C.

- **Residency Permit C**
  Non-Swiss residents who hold this permit are as near to full Swiss citizenship as they can be. With this, they are allowed to change jobs or places of residence at will. Again, it is renewable on a five-year basis, but its renewal is virtually a formality.

Another possibility for EC/EFTA passport holders is the G Permit, which allows one to work in Switzerland while living across the border. Many thousands of people who work in Lugano, Chiasso, Basel, Lausanne or Geneva live in Italy, Germany or France and cross the border daily to go to their well-paid jobs. The permit is initially given out for one year, then on a five-year renewable basis. You can have a *pied-à-terre* in Switzerland and an official place of residence across the border, but you are expected to officially reside in the latter.

Non-European Passport Holders

If you hold a passport from a non-European country, you can enter Switzerland and stay for up to three months with simply a valid passport. You will not, however, be allowed to work. While a visa is not required for many countries, the best way to find out if you need one is to get in touch with the nearest Swiss consulate. The visa normally takes one week to obtain.

It is certain that since the Schengen Agreement, entry for non-European passport holders has become more difficult. The structure is the same as for European passport holders—with short-term L permits, B permits and C permits—but your future employer has to prove that no Swiss or European national can do the job you have applied for. This rule is obviously more elastic the higher up in the echelons you go—you are less likely to get employment as a factory worker than as a company executive or a university lecturer, for example. But the arrangement remains a cumbersome one even for high-level employment.

Another difference is that whereas EU or EFTA nationals are entitled to set up a business in Switzerland (of course within the framework of Swiss business law and at your own risk), for a non-European, on the other hand, the process is far more complicated, and you would probably have to get in touch with a specialist to be able to set up a self-employed situation for yourself.

Keep in mind that a similar distinction applies to the acquisition of property in the country.

Refugees

Switzerland is pretty brutal, as are the countries around it, with its list of countries from which refugees might be accepted at any given moment (usually war zones) and has in place a policy of attempting to pacify conflicts in these countries to avoid mass immigration. It must be said that this latter component has been very seriously worked on by the foreign affairs ministry in recent years, with ambitious multilateral initiatives for peace and reconstruction under way in Kosovo, Israel, Palestine and certain regions of Africa.

But if you somehow arrive at a Swiss border crossing with a suitcase, you will be referred to the refugee authorities and your case will be assessed according to very strict criteria. You will be given minimal housing and food, and not allowed to work, while your application is examined. The majority of cases are rejected. Those who have lost or destroyed their papers get particularly rough treatment during the processing of their requests.

Some people go 'underground'—very difficult in a country as regimented as Switzerland, where the cities do not really have the population mass to absorb people unobserved. You may have a cousin who can put you up somewhere, and find you a low-level job to stay alive, but sooner or later, if you have an accident, fall ill or get into trouble, the system could well catch up with you and get others into trouble as well. You could be badly worked over, especially if you are a woman. The mafias of nightclubs and prostitution work as nastily here as elsewhere.

FIXED ABODES

By tradition, every canton and every municipality has its own list of inhabitants and its own local and state tax structure and electoral roll. If you are Swiss and you move from Aarau to Bern, say, you have to pick up your resident papers in the city hall of the former and have them transferred to and duly stamped by the city hall in the latter, becoming in the process a *confédéré* or *Eidgenoss* living in the technically foreign territory of another 'republic'. Under Swiss federal law, a citizen's residence in any place is considered as a right; but if you do not register with the authorities, you are in an illegal situation.

As a foreigner, your stay in Switzerland also entails your registration as an alien in the place you choose to live in, usually a formality if you are coming in as an employee or on a contract basis but one that you will have to look at with your employer. You will be issued a work permit and be duly registered. Naturally, as a Swiss resident, you will be paying local and federal taxes here. US citizens have a special arrangement which makes them liable for taxes in their country of origin, and if you are working for an international organisation there are also bilateral arrangements which exempt you from the bulk of local taxes. As a tax-paying resident, your children will be entitled to attend local public schools to secondary level, and the state school system—with a few local variations—works very well. (For more information, see the section 'Schooldays' in this chapter.)

You will also be compelled to join the (scandalously expensive and private) Swiss health insurance scheme which will, however, stand you in good stead in emergencies for hospitalisation and medical care. If you are here on a shorter stay or on a temporary work contract, you would be better off with an international health insurance plan. Bring the relevant documents with you as they will be asked for in case of need. Whichever system you're on, be prepared to fight for your rights—there are collectives that will help in your defence if need be.

If you come in looking for work, things get rather more complicated. The situation is again a Catch-22: without a job, you cannot get a work permit and no one is entitled to employ you legally without one. The usual thing that people who have the means do in these cases is to come in as tourists and go knocking on a few doors. (obviously you'll have been emailing and faxing resumes beforehand) and then leave temporarily while the paperwork is sorted out.

A good many people who somehow manage to sneak in across the borders from poor countries do not have this choice, and you will see them through steamy grilles on winter nights washing dishes in restaurants, doing agricultural work in far-flung villages or occasionally selling dubious and illegal things or their bodies on the sidewalks and in the bars of our cities. They are, to a large extent, at the mercy of a pretty cruel system (as they would be in most European countries) and a lurch to the right in Switzerland's political landscape has made things even more difficult for them.

It is possible in the case of a few and dwindling number of countries of origin to apply for political asylum, but the danger of that is that you will be quite quickly refused and

More and more foreigners come to Switzerland for work and leisure, such as these Tibetan visitors in Lausanne Railway Station.

tossed back across the border, or put on a chartered flight back to where you came from—in handcuffs. In the period of waiting for your hearing, you will be assigned to a grim residence and not be allowed to work. At the moment, different cantons and different cities are trying to make the system a little more human, but the federal iron fist on this situation is implacable and the fight is an uphill one.

For both this class of migrants and more orthodox ones, there are local groups of citizens and expatriates who will do their utmost to help you regularise your situation. You'll find a few addresses in the Resource Guide at the end of this book.

Accommodation: Your Place or Mine?

Switzerland is a land of rented accommodation. For most people (about 60–80 per cent) and depending on the region, it simply isn't worth buying a place to live—even modest apartments command astronomical prices. Flats in a housing block on a long-term renewable lease are a popular and usually perfectly satisfactory answer. For shorter-term rental periods, you might find a furnished or even a serviced apartment, but these are rather costly solutions in a country where a few sticks of simple furniture wouldn't set you back much.

Flats vary considerably in rent, depending on the city or town you live in, the area you choose (e.g. an old town with mountain views or an industrial suburb with a meatpacker in your backyard) and the size and quality of the lodging. In some places, such as Zürich or Geneva, flats are barely available at realistic prices, and if you are planning a work stay there, you'd be well-advised to see whether your employer has any accommodation in reserve, at least for the first few months. A colleague at the art school commuted every weekend for nearly a year from Geneva (no housing) to Basel (nice spacious flat at a reasonable price) to be with his family. In the bigger cities, a surprisingly large number of younger people live in illegal or semi-legal conditions, ranging from unofficial sublets to squats, often in buildings whose owners have gone bankrupt or which are awaiting demolition or renewal.

At the quieter end is sub-sidised housing of various kinds, often in the suburbs, to which you can get access if your income is below average for the size of your household. This usually entails going on waiting lists and presenting tax returns—and there'll be difficulties if your personal or combined income rises above the agreed limit. In most places, a minimum residency of two years is required before you can be listed for a subsidised flat—another catch-22 situation.

If someone offers you a sublet, you'd be well-advised to have an agreement made up; and you should arrange with the tenant to let the owner or the housing

Squatting

Some squats last for years, allowing groups of residents to come to agreements with the building owners—often banks who have repossessed blocks with defaulted mortgages, and are pleased to have the building given a modicum of security. I have gone to concerts, movies and plays in some of Geneva's squats, which form part of the 'alternative' cultural scene. My bicycle repair shop and favourite second-hand bookshop are both in buildings that have been squatted in for years and are now occupied by arrangement with the city administration, who owns them. Other squats are somewhat less than salubrious, though these are often still pretty congenial, with music and a rather lively social scene in the evenings—typically passed in a haze of sweet smoke.

agent know. By sublet, obviously, I mean that someone lets you have their place for a limited period of time, e.g. while they are on an overseas posting, at the same conditions they have it at, and in return, you will secure their lease and defray expenses in their absence. If the tenant tries to let you a place at a much higher amount than they're paying themselves (and you can ask to look at their rent slips), you are obviously being unfairly exploited.

Flat hunting is much like anywhere else. Looking for a place starts with work notice boards and the newspapers—get these early as competition is usually quite fierce. There are accommodation agencies too, and you can look at their offers and be listed there. Some of them take the equivalent of about a month's rent if you find your ideal place. This is illegal but difficult to enforce especially in places where there is a housing shortage. In general, rent is monthly, and the utilities and heating are charged separately, the one by the power and gas board, the others directly by the housing agent. The latter is obliged to show you receipts if you challenge the charges, though in these days of expensive gas and oil, these can understandably be pretty steep.

The owner of the building, or his agent, will probably ask you for anything up to three months' rent in advance, and this amount will be escrowed in a blocked bank account until you leave the apartment. When you move in, you must insist on a full tour of the place and you must note, with the owner or agent, any damage or wear and tear to the place, as he or she will certainly notice any of same when you move out and hold you liable for payment for any repairs or redecoration from the blocked rent money, which is his or her right. In this context I have found that having a household insurance with a liability clause quite useful. Personally, I've used it twice when I left apartments, once for a wrinkled body carpet for which the landlord blamed me, the other time for a curious paint stain in the attic of an older place.

Obviously it pays to be careful when you sign a lease. Get it read over by someone who is familiar with such documents to make sure that no one is trying to pull the wool over your eyes. Most cantons have standard lease formulations available, but then again with the housing shortage in some places, unscrupulous and even criminal

owners will try to inflict unacceptable conditions on you, knowing full well that if you refuse, the next person will grab the place.

Your power and gas connections are easily arranged. In a normal situation, the (publicly owned) utilities will have left a card there which you will see when you first arrive, and the connections and accounts can usually be arranged within 24 hours. If you have left another place with unpaid bills, you are, of course, asking for trouble as these records are carefully kept.

Telephone connections are a little more complicated. The industry has been considerably diversified, with a handful of private suppliers alongside that of the national 'Swiss Telecomm' and some of them have interesting offers, above all in the field of international calls. The tendency these days is that most newcomers come in with their mobile phones which, if the operator is a major one (e.g. Orange, Vodaphone), they can adapt to the national one to avoid paying too much for local calls. They can then take a little more time to shop around for a fixed apartment line and see what the different operators are proposing. All operators offer an Internet frequency (ADSL) at reasonable prices.

Most apartment leases are tacitly renewable every year for a limited number of years (often three). Should you wish to leave before the lease runs out, it is your responsibility to find new tenants—solvent and respectable—for your flat.

Subletting without telling the owner and his agent is generally prohibited, and you do it at your own risk and peril. It would mean, quite simply, that you would be financially and legally liable should the sub-lessee do any damage to the property or fail to pay rent and charges regularly. He or she could also be thrown out if the proprietor or agent has not agreed to the arrangement beforehand—leaving you without an apartment.

If you run into any trouble with housing agreements, most cantons have one or several tenant protection associations that can advise you (usually for the modest price of an annual membership fee). If need be they will take up your case against finagling threats or expulsions with a great deal of integrity and energy. The justifications for terminating your lease, increasing your rent or attempting to expel you are written into laws which, in the main, are quite fair and balanced, and which Swiss magistrates will usually enforce pretty strictly. In Geneva and in most other cantons, there is a special court to hear such conflicts, with one representative of the proprietors and one from the tenant association—usually both lawyers, or someone well-versed in tenancy law—sitting on the bench with the magistrate.

Keeping the Money and Renting

Many people here who could afford to buy an apartment or a house rent quite modest housing. Their spare money will be spent on holidays, or occasionally on holiday places, or other houses far from Switzerland. A surprising number of people here have a place in the mountains or, in the case of migrant workers, they'll often be building a house in their country of origin, be it Portugal, Croatia or Turkey. I've been shown many photographs of sumptuous half-finished villas in more or less exotic settings by colleagues, cleaning ladies and hospital staff hailing from all corners of the world.

A lot of local people we know seem to have a chalet, or occasionally an apartment in a chalet, which they have bought for a relatively low price and which they may lend to friends in the off-peak season, and rent out during the high season, while using it for their own holidays. Others rent or buy shares in tiny houses in collective gardens on the edges of cities—often funded by co-operatives or trade unions (Schrebergarten or Jardins Familiaux)—where they spend the fine months growing broccoli, berries and beans, and sitting out in the evening with a barbecue and a glass of wine, seemingly far from the teeming cities.

If a friend or colleague offers you the use of such a place, make sure you contribute in some way. You could offer him the rent, or the charges (electricity, heating in winter, etc.), or at the very least, leave something for the owner when you move on. And by that I don't mean half a rusting tin of ravioli growing whiskers in his fridge, but rather a couple of bottles of wine neatly stashed away in the wine corner.

There is also a market for apartments and houses for sale, of course. Prices, as I have mentioned, are high by the standards of most countries, though regional variations are quite marked. Mortgages, on the other hand, tend to carry quite low interest, so it is possible to carry quite a large mortgage for many years paying barely more than you would in rent and having the advantage of paying off your own place.

You would still have to be considering a longish residency here to buy a place. It is virtually impossible to buy a Swiss property if you are a foreign national residing out of the country, and you should have a qualified lawyer look at the law relating to this before you make any move in this direction. (There is, naturally, an exception made for holiday places, and a lot of foreigners own a place in the mountains or timeshare a slice of a chalet, enabling them to have a *pied-à-terre* of their own for holidays.)

Some cantons are, however, more open to foreign property buyers than others, particularly those in the more touristic parts; the map on http://www.rellox.com/buying-a-property-in-switzerland gives an up-to-date indication of this. In all cases, transactions must take place in Swiss currency, and are subject to Swiss property law.

You must, of course, add an allowance for maintenance to your costs. In housing blocks, there is usually a caretaker or a cleaning service to pay, and money has to be put aside for more important structural repairs that the building will require in time. In private houses, you should also have some money set aside, as the municipal charges for things like waste water connections and other services fall on property owners.

BANKING

To open a Swiss bank account, you would usually be required to show proof of your identity and nationality, and proof of Swiss residency, a *permis d'établissement* or *Niederlassungsbewilligung* (love the German habit of stringing words together!) from the state immigration service where you are settled.

Most current accounts come with a coded card in your name, which allow you to draw cash and make certain payments anywhere in Europe, and in many other places

Numbered accounts are a service Swiss banks provide, where your account has only a number and a code known solely to the management of the bank. Again this is something you should see about with the bank you go to.

too. Different accounts are available, as elsewhere: savings and salary accounts designed for a regular income and payments, and commercial accounts more suited to absorbing big credits and debits with minimum fuss.

If you leave Switzerland and want to leave your account open, you'd better check with the bank manager first. For most countries, it is possible; for some, it may cause fiscal and administrative difficulties.

I'M THE TAXMAN

Taxes—boring stuff, but important if you find yourself working in Switzerland for any length of time. If you have a diplomatic posting or you work for an international agency, you won't really have to worry—there are bilateral arrangements which exempt you from paying taxes in Switzerland. You will, of course, have to pay the VAT on normal purchases, although for major things, say a car or a washing machine, you may be able to get that back. The nice person in your company's human-resource department should be able to tell you about that. VAT in Switzerland, moreover, is much less than in EEC countries.

For shorter-term work, you'll be taxed at the source— with a sum withheld from your salary. In any case, a social security and unemployment contribution is automatically deducted from your salary. Also deducted is a contribution to a compulsory federal retirement fund (AHV or AVS), which, if you are definitely quitting Switzerland you are entitled to reclaim. This can amount to quite a tidy sum after a few years!

However, if you stay for a longer period, you will be considered a resident using local amenities and infrastructure, and will hence be subject to Swiss tax law and come under the steely glare of the tax department. Swiss taxes are probably not excessively high but they are rather complicated. The taxing is at three levels: local, cantonal and federal. The actual administration of what you have to pay lies in the hands of the cantonal authorities. A beautifully presented bundle of papers (with a CD and an Internet site thrown in) will arrive in your post box in February, to be filled in by the end of March. This is available in Switzerland's three major languages, and in English too in most places. It will have on it your matriculation number—which you will also find on your grey card of entitlement to the national superannuation fund. The income of the previous calendar year is the tax basis for state tax, so if you're earning, you'd be wise to deposit a part of your salary in a blocked account to be covered when the first bill arrives. The sums can be pretty stiff, and your employer should be able to give you a good idea of the percentage that the municipal, state and federal tax will add up to so you will know how much to squirrel away for the taxman.

Tax Deductions

You are entitled to a variety of deductions, which you must carefully fill in on the tax form. These deductions vary from canton to canton, but remain constant for the federal taxes—so you'll be filling in a double-column declaration. The municipal tax is usually a percentage (about 30–50 per cent) of the cantonal tax.

If you have an important income in your country of origin, you'd be well-advised to see a tax consultant (*Treuhand* or *fiduciaire*) and talk it through with him, having already seen to the matter before you migrate so as to have good documentation.

If you are married under a common arrangement (without a contract for the separation of your property), you will be able to deduct a sum off one of the spouse's earnings. Children under 18 in your household (whether you are married or not), or for whom you are financially responsible up to 24 years of age, also entitle you to an income deduction. Other deductions can be claimed for personal insurances (life and health), transport fees, special work clothes and medical fees. Money contributed to the AHV/AVS retirement fund, your work-based fund and any private fund you may belong to can also be deducted from taxes within certain limits.

If you are here in a less than legal way, you will have to find a place to live with a friend, as it would be risky to have your name on a door or a letterbox. It is not easy to regularise your situation in such cases, and you would have to apply for an asylum-seeker status (which, as elsewhere in Europe, is pretty hellish, with no right to work, assigned residency in barracks, endless administrative and judicial hassles and the risk of expulsion hanging over you) or simply try to stay clandestine, which, believe me, is extremely difficult in a small and rather xenophobic country, the more so if your foreignness is written in your face or the way you speak.

The whole tax liability thing is based on the concept of residency (*Niederlassung* for our Swiss-German friends, *séjour* in the French-speaking part). This will entail going to the municipal offices and having your papers made out. If you have come here on an employment contract, your employer will have arranged a work permit for you, and you will need to present that and your passport or other proof of citizenship. It is very difficult to find work without a valid permit and very few employers have the clout to get these for you. These papers must be surrendered when you leave the country.

IN SICKNESS AND IN HEALTH

In general, if you can afford it, the Swiss health-care system works well, with a large number of general practitioners, specialists and dentists in relation to the population.

Even if you are not comfortable in German, Italian or French, you will be able find a doctor that speaks your language, be it English, Persian, Mandarin or Magyar.

Health-care is, however, far too expensive, as it is run by a cartel of private insurance companies (*Krankenkassen* or *caisses-maladie*) that have grown out of co-operatives and are now in a very powerful lobbying position. Their service offers are rigorously identical right throughout the field and they are strictly controlled by a federal commission which they, however, seem to be overly represented on. Prices of the monthly contribution vary from canton to canton based on a complicated actuary and cost-of-living calculation. Different companies also offer different tariffs and there is always a rush to the cheapest one each year as the (inevitable) annual increases in tariffs are announced.

In most health insurance, you will have to pay the first

few treatments on a franchise system before the subsidy kicks in, and you'd be wise to do a few calculations before opting for any particular scheme. For instance, I am on a 600-franc annual franchise at the moment, and I rarely cover it (touch wood!) as I have comparatively little to do with medical folk. But this saves me about 750 francs a year in monthly payments.

Maybe one day health insurance will be nationalised as it is in France, Canada and the UK and people will pay a rate according to their income, but (as a militant fighting on that front) I know that it's a long battle. At the moment, if you have four children and a normal decent income, you're in trouble. There are subsidies available at the cantonal level but they are very difficult to obtain. The canton I live in, although reasonably generous in other fields, is obviously fighting for every scrap of paper to avoid paying out what people are entitled to.

Hospital fees are covered on a similar basis and there, the insurance can stand you in good stead as a difficult operation or a stint in intensive care can cost you the price of a small house. Hospitals are generally publicly owned and managed on a cantonal level. We have found the service to be fair and correct, with highly competent medical and nursing staff, quite edible institutional meals, and reasonable access to rooms and services.

We did, on the other hand, pay more into our health insurance a couple of decades ago, to entitle my wife to have our two children in a private clinic with a slightly more luxurious room and access to her gynaecologist who practised there.

Fees

Doctor's tariffs are fixed nationally according to a draconian system called Tarmed which entails filling out or ticking off on a highly complicated form every pulse taken, every auscultation on the stethoscope and every stitch put in your injured finger.

Alternative medicine is very much available here, but read the small print on your health insurance contract carefully. It is not always reimbursed. The fairest system seems to be one where you name a personal or family doctor who is listed with your assurance, and who can then refer you to an osteopath acupuncturist or some other alternative specialist.

This would be a kind of guarantee for the insurance and assure their participation.

Swiss dentists are no different from their Australian, Indian or Kenyan counterparts in that they care for your teeth as best they can. But they cost five times as much. So if you are not here permanently, take that major dental operation back home with you!

SCHOOLDAYS

If you come to Switzerland for a longer stay and you bring your children along, you'll find a good range of educational facilities open to you. The choices you make will depend largely on your own wishes and plans, but the Swiss public education system does produce very good results in most places, and education is a function taken very seriously by the various local and state administrations whose constitutional duty it is to supply it.

One drawback, which is quickly becoming less important as harmonisation policies are implemented, is the difference in curricula between different cantons, which has been known to make transfers at secondary or tertiary levels rather awkward as the various institutions search for equivalents between the different state qualifications. A federal *maturité*, a kind of high school diploma which is gained at age 18 or so, would be a good qualification to consider if you plan to be in different parts of Switzerland.

Private Schools

You may, of course, be here for a shorter period and feel that it is important that your offspring continue their education in the language and academic environment you'll be going back to. If such is the case, in most of the bigger centres, you will find a private network of international schools from elementary to high-school level, where lessons are dispensed in the languages and curricula of most European and North American countries.

The International School of Geneva, as one example, prepares students to pre-university level with the option of English, French or bilingual studies. Examinations proposed are the Cambridge Higher Certificate, the American Board of Universities entrance or the French Baccalaureate, as well as the Swiss federal Maturité. A private German high school is also available which gets students to the Abschlussprüfung level, as are religion-based schools for Jewish and Muslim students. Rudolf Steiner and Maria Montessori both have exciting holistic educational systems to propose, and have been established in Switzerland for almost a century. Their modern schools are still an option in the bigger Swiss centres. All of these private systems are, naturally, fee-paying, although the fees are often tax-deductible.

Public Schools

Swiss public schooling consists of a compulsory nine years (Standard One to Nine) but most children start earlier, with up to two years of preschool. After the ninth mandatory year, many go on to a series of high schools or take an apprenticeship which will also include a minimum of two weekdays at a technical school. The system is a good and fair one, with much emphasis placed on the teaching of tolerance and responsibility, and in most cases, generally enthusiastic staff, backed by more or less supportive parent organisations at lower levels. School buildings and facilities are usually very good, and, being provided by the municipalities, are a matter of local pride. Education is, by law, free of charge to tax-paying residents, so it's not surprising that it takes the largest share on most state budget expenses. If you are on a tax-exempt stay (e.g. international agency, diplomat, etc), bilateral arrangements are usually in place to allow your children to use the system.

School hours vary quite a bit from canton to canton. Local primary schools run from about 8:30 am to about 4:00 pm, with a generous one-and-a-half-hour lunch break during which the little cherubs usually go home for a bite to eat. Schools in larger centres have canteens where the children of working parents get a good meal for a reasonable payment.

The Parents' Association

At primary school level, there are often quite active parents' associations, definitely worth joining if you're a new arrival and want to find your way around and make new friends while making yourself useful. You can be involved in organising school trips, extensions of services like sport and school lunches, and occasionally lobbying authorities for necessary changes of organisation.

After Standard Six, students attend junior high for three years and these are variously named *Mittelschule*, *Collège* or *Cycle d'Orientation* depending on the canton you're in. After that, they spend another three years at college (*Kantonalschule*, *Collège*, *Handelsschule*, *Ecole de Commerce*, etc) or at a commercial or trade school, which will bring them to Maturité level, usually attained at about 18 years of age.

Further on, there are centres of higher learning (*Fachhochschulen* or *Haute Ecoles Spécialisés*) which train students to higher qualifications in business, trades, arts and professions, and, of course, a pretty impressive university system. These are, again, usually open to all for a reasonable enrolment fee—the Swiss have not gone down the road of privatising higher education, and see educational institutions as a public service rather than as a milch cow for the private sector to enrich itself. The advent of the Bologna rules will change a few of these precepts, but it will also enable students much greater mobility between higher learning institutions in different countries. The Erasmus system, already in place, allows me to work with students from all corners of eastern and western Europe, as well as from Canada, which might make teaching more demanding at times but certainly more stimulating for all concerned.

TRANSPORT
The Best Trains In The World

Not very large, densely populated and topographically varied, Switzerland is the ideal country for intensive passenger rail development, and the challenge has been superbly taken up. The country boasts the densest national railway network in the world, as well as one of the best efficiency and safety records. The network started as a number of small private projects but the main lines have been nationalised with the standard European gauge for close to a century now. The frenzy for privatisation seems to have passed us by, and the service is still essentially a government-owned public corporation. It would be madness for any private enterprise to take on an infrastructure of such complexity, let alone to try to turn a profit on an institution which is mainly there to serve the public and decongest the overloaded road network. It was, thanks to the massive production of hydro-power, the first network in the world to be completely electrified, and the phrase 'run like a Swiss train' still holds true, the occasional lapse notwithstanding.

The Swiss Federal Railways (SBB, CFF or FFS, depending on your lingo) has several times won the Brunel award—

High-speed trains provide connections between major Swiss cities.

given by the foundation named after the great Franco-British engineer—for excellence in railway design, and its new interurban and suburban trains are certainly at a level with the best Europe can offer.

On the sinuous western line, a new unit train of Swiss-Italian design has the capacity of leaning into curves like a motorcycle, increasing speeds by about 25–30 per cent without impairing passenger comfort. It also gives a vivid Porsche-like sensation of acceleration. Double-storey trains with very pleasant interiors whisper along the main diagonal and transalpine lines between the big urban centres.

The Swiss railway network has also won the Wakker Foundation's prize for its policy of preserving the quality of its architectural and civil engineering installations. There have been some beautiful restorations of older stations: Zürich's extension to take in the underground S-Bahn, for example, and the very fine work in Lausanne and Baden.

Life on the Trains

A crazy project called Swissmetro was mooted several years ago that proposed a 500-km/h pneumatic underground system to link the two corners of Switzerland through the main centres in less than 30 minutes. An ambitious plan, though it would seem a bit of a pity to miss out on the lovely scenic views of tidy Swiss landscapes and mountains as one ambles along at a leisurely 160–200 km/h. However, for most Swiss, this is simply a very convenient and safe way of getting around between cities and towns.

Business people will not hesitate to get up at six in the morning to zip from Chur to Basel for a board meeting at 9:00 am, knowing that a comfortable wagon awaits them in which they can choose either normal seats or, if they are in a group, an upstairs circular arrangement where they can chat around a coffee table and get down to some preparatory work.

Students are often quietly curled up with a bottle of bubbly water and a sheaf of notes or working on their portable computers as they travel from Bern to Fribourg on the morning train. Functionaries are sitting in a group in the restaurant car coming home from Bienne to Zürich, talking over the day's policy meeting with a tea or a coke in front of them. A discreetly rowdy group of uniformed soldiers takes up half a compartment, their packs and rifles neatly stacked behind their seats, cans of beer on the little tables in front of them as they swap military jokes of dubious taste.

In the first-class wagon, a national councillor from Aarau is on his way to Bern, his telephone clapped to his ear as he converses in brisk Swiss-German with a party colleague. Grandmothers are herding grandchildren into a special play wagon, and a family of Indian tourists are looking out enthralled at the vista of late afternoon sun reflected off Lake Geneva as the inter-city train snakes silently down through the vines towards Lausanne. Beside them a couple of farmers from the Valais are checking their tickets from Geneva Airport where a modern rail-air terminal awaits them to catch their flight to Athens for a well-earned holiday.

Students curl up with their notes and work on their portable computers as they travel by train.

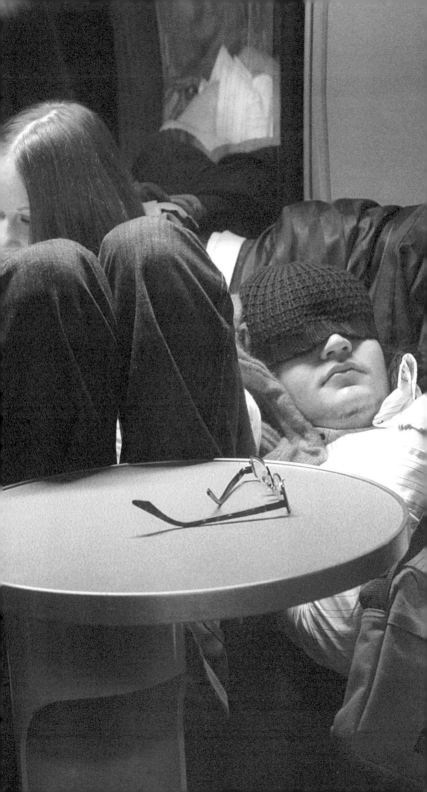

Fares are rather expensive, so it pays to shop around for possible reductions if you're planning a longer stay. Family cards are available which allow children under 14 to travel free with their parents. There are also student cards, as well as Platform 7 cards for those under 26 years of age that for an annual fee entitle them to free travel from 7:00 pm to 7:00 am. For a rather steeper price, you can also get a demi-tarif card which allows you to travel for half-price. It costs 160 francs a year—though this goes down to 135 if you combine it with a Visa card—but it's well worth it, the more so as it gives you reductions on the whole gamut of public transport.

But trains are not the only form of transport in Switzerland, nor are they the only mode that is so efficient. The other day I had to go to Zürich for a day. The normal fare is 170 francs but using my demi- tarif card, I only paid half. Then I took a day pass for 57 francs, which also entitled me to public transport in any Swiss town. It was great. I'd brought copious quantities of paper—various reports and minutes of commissions I

The *mouette* water bus is one of the many options in Geneva's public transport system.

hadn't got round to reading—and a novel, in case I got bored. It was a journey of over three hours, and gave me time to reflect ruefully that I could have been in Paris in the same lapse of time. In Zürich, I clambered aboard an elderly but friendly tram that was almost rattle-free, and rode out to the trade fair hall to look at stuff and talk turkey to people. Later, I found a smart low-floored bus at the door and took a short hop to the suburban station where a modern two-level S-train (suburban train, run by a consortium of the Swiss railways and the publicly-owned Zürich transport system) arrived within three minutes and whisked me back to the central station in five.

Baby, You Can Drive My Car

Switzerland has too many cars for a small country, all the more so as it is also used as a means of access to other European countries. The Gotthard tunnel is blocked up by heavy traffic in the holiday season. Trucks by the hundreds rumble through Switzerland on the Germany-Austria-Italy route, polluting the approaches of the tunnel with their stink and noise.

For these latter using Switzerland as a transit, a new solution is being pioneered where entire trucks, or alternatively their integral loads, are rail-freighted across the country. The solution is a costly one, and still not fully implemented, but it looks as though it might eventually lead to some reduction in traffic.

This being the case, Switzerland still has horrendously high car-registration figures, and there is pressure on the country to ease up on road building and let the environment breathe a little. On the other side of the fence, there is a powerful car lobby clamouring for more roads.

Parking in the big cities is a major hassle too. In Geneva and certain other centres, residents are now given special stickers entitling them to parking privileges in the blue zones of their local area. More recently, housing blocks are compelled by law to have underground garages for the residents. If you have to take a car into a city, you can easily

Traffic in Swiss cities can get heavy when it snows. Be extra careful when driving in these conditions.

spend 30–40 francs feeding parking meters, going into public underground car parks or simply paying fines. I personally put a 50-franc surcharge on bills from my bureau if I have to transport materials by car in the inner city, and none of my clients has ever raised a corporate eyebrow.

Swiss roads are generally well-maintained, with a national—partly motorway—network; a cantonal network, initiated and cared for by state administrations; and municipal roads in most towns.

The national motorway network is pretty good, considering the enormous engineering difficulties in some regions, not to mention the acrimonious 'Not in my backyard'-style political conflicts every major project in Switzerland entails. It is financed, in part, by a compulsory tax which all motorway users pay once a year. It costs 40 francs at present, and you get a natty coloured sticker on your windscreen. The police do not usually bother to check these systematically, but you can be busted for the tax when you're driving into Switzerland through a motorway border post, and you'll certainly get a whacking fine if you run into any other kind of trouble on a motorway without it and the police are present.

Renting a Car

Rental cars are available, with similar conditions as elsewhere in Europe, and trans-European rentals are easily arranged if you are, say, driving to Munich or Brussels and flying home. You can also rent small vans for moving stuff (up to 3 tonnes with a normal driver's licence) or camper vans (rather costly—shop round a bit using the Yellow Pages or Internet) in most big centres. It seems to be impossible to rent a car in Switzerland without a valid international credit card.

Driver's licences? Best have your own converted into an international one, which can then be reissued as a Swiss one if you choose to reside here. Driver's licences (and dog licences) are issued by the canton administrations, to persons over 18. You will get into big trouble if you're caught in a driving incident without one.

Getting a driver's licence here entails sitting for a strict theory and practical test—not easy if your language skills are not yet great. Most people take at least some lessons from a driving school; this helps even if you have driven a fair bit as there will be foibles and small things you may overlook which the inspector will pounce on.

Traffic rules and signs in Switzerland are much like those in the other European countries around them, the closest equivalent being Germany. Cars drive on the right-hand side. Unlike Germany, though, the Swiss have a motorway speed limit of 120 km/h (75mph), which is sometimes lowered in difficult conditions (heavy traffic, snow, etc) by luminous signposting. Patrolling is done on a state police level.

Highway speeds are limited to a sluggish 80 km/h (50 mph), but many cantons do not enforce this too rigorously. You will soon see how your canton deals with it. No one is ever stopped for minor speeding in the Valais I'm told; on the other hand, in some of the tiny, densely populated Swiss-German cantons, you'd never get the opportunity to accelerate above 80 km/h (50 mph) before the next wee village flecks up. In villages and towns, the limit is 50 km/h (31 mph) although occasionally it drops to 40 km/h (25 mph) or even 30 km/h (18.6 mph) in the feeder network of residential areas. Watch out for cameras and radars, which are usually housed in large, tombstone-like structures on the roadside, and sometimes in police cars neatly parked by the road, often unmarked.

Fines are very high indeed, and repeat offenders are hit a double whammy—in the pocket book and by a revocation of their driving permit. There are stories of speed-freaks having their Porsches and Ferraris confiscated by implacable cops after a dash at 275 km/h (170 mph) late at night, and finishing the night in the slammer. I've mentioned that driving with alcohol (0.5 promille) and under the influence of drugs is also very severely punished and would, in most cases, also have a few months' licence-withdrawal as part of the penalty.

Want to buy a car, or bring one in with you? No great problem, if you have residence in Switzerland. If you choose to bring your car in, you'll have to pay the federal TVA (8 per cent) on it, which you can have deducted in the country you are exporting from (lots of paperwork but it can save you money, Swiss purchase taxes being very high) and it will have to go through a technical control before being matriculated and issued with number plates and a 'grey card' by the state in which you reside.

Car prices seem a little higher here than in most neighbouring countries. Insurance on a third-party level is compulsory, with considerable no-claim bonuses if you have an incident-free few years. A full insurance cover can be quite pricey; personally, I've always driven 'elderly' cars so I've never bothered lumbering myself with one.

If you come from a country where people drive on the left, driving on the 'wrong side of the road' might take some getting use to. Very likely you will be spending the initial months peering out to see what's going on ahead when your controls are on the right-hand side. You may also have some difficulty with parts for certain British makes, as an eccentric friend of mine who sported a three-wheeled Bond Minicar discovered. Exhaust-emission standards are more severe and more rigorously enforced in Switzerland than in other European countries'—another thing worth keeping in mind if you're importing an older car from a less fussy country. For those who will be in Switzerland for less than a year, a special licensing system with number plates marked with a red stripe applies.

State Vehicle Tax

There is an annual state licence fee based on the taxable horse-power, worked out on the cubic capacity of the vehicle.

What do the Swiss drive? European and Asian cars in about equal proportions, with a few American ones thrown in for good measure. Big American cars, though, can present certain parking and driving problems in the picturesque older parts of Swiss towns. The major European and Asian manufacturers are all very well represented here in terms of sales, service and spare parts. Unlike Switzerland's bigger neighbours, there is virtually no Swiss car industry, and there seems little feeling that the European makers need our support. Nevertheless, there seems to be a large proportion of Opels, Volkswagens, Audis and BMWs in the German part, and many Renaults, Citroëns and Peugeots in the Romande region. It might have something to do with the culture, or perhaps it's the advertising on TV which knows no borders. My Swiss-Italian friend drives an Alfa Romeo on weekends and a Fiat for work. The best-selling model throughout Switzerland in the last few years has been the Volkswagen Golf, ideally suited to the purse and lifestyle of the Swiss, reasonably economical (fuel is expensive here too) and not too 'flashy'.

Bringing Your Car

Some people bring their cars when they come here, a good idea if the vehicle is a left-hand drive and is in good condition. It will have to pass customs and also go through a technical check-up which is pretty thorough and strict here. If you go to France, Italy or Germany to buy a new or recent car (at prices below Swiss ones), you'll also have to do your paperwork before you go. The Swiss automobile club, Touring, could advise you on that.

Along with many people I know, I buy my cars second-hand. The Swiss are, on the whole, pretty meticulous, and they like the latest in all things, so there is a good second-hand car market at affordable (albeit still high) prices. Any used car on the market has to have been through the very rigorous Swiss roadworthiness checks 30 days before the sale, so if you buy a mainstream vehicle, you'll probably get a pretty good run. This control is obligatory every three years, and there are comparatively few old cars on the roads in Switzerland. Our very comfortable 12-year-old Citroën Diesel is definitely among the scruffier and older cars in the region we live in, though this is scarcely a worry to us as we rumble off to the shopping mall or wind along a mountain road with a stack of skis and snowboards on the roof rack.

For motorcycles and scooters, the pattern is the same, with the additional factor that machines of over 125 cc are restricted to people over the age of 20. Scooters have become very popular as a form of individual transport in the cities and suburbs.

Urban Switzerland, with its small compact cities, is pretty well adapted for bicycles, and you can get around the towns very quickly by using bicycle lanes and occasionally (illegally!) bus lanes to snake past the traffic. Most drivers won't run you over—it's too much trouble. Do watch out for tramlines— horrible traps for narrow wheels. You are recommended, although not legally obliged, to wear a protective helmet. You pay a small annual fee for a bicycle number plate, which covers you for insurance purposes, and can help if your mount gets pinched; in urban areas, bicycle thieves are a major plague. Pedal softly and carry a big padlock and chain—to paraphrase Teddy Roosevelt.

SHOPPING
The range of goods available here is probably on a par with most civilised countries, although there are bits and pieces I'll find in Paris, Milan or London (respectively kitchen gear, hats and books) in a far bigger range of choices.

The first myth—that is no longer really true—is that Switzerland is much more expensive than other places. Swiss francs will buy a lot, but the problem is that Swiss francs are rather pricey to acquire. So if you're earning money locally, there is not going to be a great problem in shopping with it. On the other hand, if you come in with almost any foreign currency except for Japanese yen, you'll find the buying power of what you have far less than in the country you've earned it in. In the latter case, you'll have to be pretty careful, making calculations back to your own currency to see whether a deal is worth it. Even then you will find some items at good prices—watches, hi-fi equipment, computers, accessories.

The Swiss sales tax at 8 per cent is (for the moment) lower than that of the European bloc, and outlets are ferociously competitive, so this allows for some interesting over-the-counter prices.

If you are a Swiss resident, you can get a reduction of the European VAT for items bought here against paying the Swiss one, which is worth your while for expensive purchases, although it does entail a certain amount of paperwork and hanging around at the border customs offices. Similar arrangements can be made if you order goods from overseas through the Internet, where more expensive items will, in any case, have to be declared and taxed at customs. If you don't declare it, customs will bill you for it either on delivery or beforehand if the sum is important.

Larger items—cars, houses and so on—have historically been far more expensive than in surrounding countries.

Used But Still Good

Incidentally, Switzerland is a very interesting place to buy used goods. If you know what you want and what you're buying, you will find many relatively new items in the automotive, photographic, music, video and IT categories here which have been carefully looked after and are offered at good prices in good condition, often with the original guarantee still in force. One explanation for this is the Swiss passion for having the latest model of everything, which as we know doesn't always mean the best.

So what can you get? A friend who loves music picked up a 30-year-old Steinway piano at a good price through an ad in the local paper. As a professional photographer, I have bought most of my non-digital cameras and accessories in the same way through advertisements or the Internet.

Cycling is a popular means of getting around. Parents with toddlers may simply attach a baby wagon to their bicycle.

The Swiss Red Cross runs superb second-hand clothes stores, far removed from the jumble shops of a decade ago. Now they've moved upmarket and are selling clean, good-quality stuff through small shops all over Swiss towns. Prices are still very interesting, and the nice suit I bought that way cost me perhaps a fifth of the price of a new item and had been well run-in by someone of roughly my own build.

Downmarket there are church- or charity-run *brocantes* or *Brockenhäuser*, which sell almost everything imaginable. They are a good source of furniture—often very respectable pieces—and the countless items you'll find useful or picturesque for your new home here. The noticeboards of big firms, international agencies or universities are also often a good source of information for second-hand wares—especially household goods—that people want to dispose of as they move on or up.

But for the majority, shopping will be done at the normal retail outlets along the main street or in shopping malls, much like anywhere else in the world. In a country where manufacturing and supplies are pretty varied, you'll have a wide choice of goods and you'll quickly find your way around different makes and levels of quality.

Clothing and shoes come in an enormous range of prices and quality, and much depends on where you do your shopping. An airport shopping mall or the flash high streets of large cities will obviously be higher priced than a suburban shopping centre or a small-town chain store.

Most people get excited when sales are on, and in some years the sales do bring remarkable bargains to light. They tend to be seasonal, in January and June/July. The January sales are often a good way to buy winter-sport equipment, which can be very expensive. Seeing as the best skiing is usually from mid-January to March, this makes quite good sense. In the last few years, there has been a considerable loosening up of the official control of sales; the bigger department stores often have specials or sales outside of the two main periods.

There is another current of sales which is worth mentioning: mail order. You will certainly get flyers in your mailbox about different bargains available for a remittance or postal payment. The bigger, more reputable houses doing this are quickly recognised by the most cautious clients and, especially when we had a young family, we picked up a lot of stuff for reasonable prices from such outlets. The fly-by-night outfits are recognisable by their garish style of publicity, their tendency to offer you monetary prizes in fictitious lotteries and all the rackets you can think of. Avoid these. Consumer monitoring groups are worth joining as they can give sound level-headed advice on these matters.

Door-to-door salespeople are a dying breed as housing becomes more and more fortified, but there again you must be very careful not to sign anything unless you are absolutely certain that you need the item proposed, that the quality of the offer is adequate, and that the price and conditions are fair. Any document you sign can be revoked within a 48-hour cooling-off period. Personally, I don't bother with telephone marketers and usually politely and firmly cut off their sales chatter.

FOOD AND ENTERTAINING

CHAPTER 6

"One more cup of coffee 'fore you go,
To the valley below"
—Bob Dylan

HOW THE SWISS FEED

The traditional Swiss pattern of meals starts early in the morning with a 'continental' breakfast—yoghurt, bread and jam, cereals of various kinds (including that fine Swiss institution of Birchermüesli), all washed down with milk, coffee or chocolate.

Most Swiss take a morning coffee break around 9 or 10 am, which might include a small snack along with a cup of coffee, either in a café or at their workplace or school. Coffee is drunk strong—albeit longer than the Italian espresso—and often with a dash of cream supplied in little capsules. The coffee break gives people a chance to look at the morning paper, and to have a little chinwag with colleagues or friends. Small bakery items— croissants, little sandwiches or even small bars of chocolate— could be nibbled as they relax.

> In Bern cafés, coffee is oddly served in stem glasses, often with a dash of plum, pear or cherry brandy.

Tea, in the Anglo-Saxon or South-Asian sense, is not something the Swiss seem to know about, and you're liable to end up with a tepid cup of teabag-muck, with a capsule of coffee cream instead of milk. (If you want a decent cup of tea, come to our place!) On the other hand, the Swiss are good at a variety of tisanes, of which the subtle Lindenblüten is a favourite. Made from lime-tree flowers, it produces a mildness of spirit and a serenity of mind ideal for attacking stubborn

Excel spreadsheets on hazy, sleepy afternoons.

Lunch, in smaller places, is a longish break of up to two hours, and was traditionally a cooked meal taken *en famille*. This would be of the meat/fish-and-two-veggies variety with bubbly water or apple juice (one of the finer Swiss drinks, by the way), after which the breadwinner would go back to work, and the kiddies back to their various schools, while mum stacked the dishwasher and got on with various chores.

Supper, taken quite early (around 6 pm, or at the latest 7 pm), would be a lighter meal—a few leftovers fried up, one of a large variety of fine soups, or a salad with cheese and cold cuts in summer.

But in the cities, this pattern has pretty much disappeared, with working couples and latchkey kids, so that now, for a lot

of Swiss, the main meal is in the evening, with a snack-like lunch improvised by those who make it home, and a day menu in the staff or school cafeteria or a nearby restaurant for those who don't. This has also made the evening meal a little later and more substantial, when everyone is more or less back from work, music lessons, sports fixtures, last-minute shopping.

The Spanish Way

Some people of southern origin have simply taken their life rhythms and eating patterns with them, and the Spanish family across the road from our apartment used to regularly sit down to huge convivial family dinners at about ten and send the kiddies to bed around one.

If you have people round for an evening meal, you'll probably want to go beyond pre-cooked pasta. A lot of Swiss go to considerable trouble to cook you something delicious which will be washed down with a bottle or two of wine. If you want to cook something exotic for your invited guests, it might be wise to give them some idea of what you're preparing. They'll probably be delighted but there's always the chance of a seafood allergy or a phobia of foods they are not familiar with.

If you're invited to a friend's for a meal, by all means bring a bottle around with you; it will be welcome. My wife and I also have many arrangements with friends where we turn up at someone's place with a plate of food if a bigger gathering is expected. If there are certain foods you cannot eat, it is considered courteous if you mention this to your host sometime before the meal. It would also be expected of the host to offer non-alcoholic drinks as an alternative to wine or beer with no questions asked and no stigma attached.

SHOPPING FOR FOOD

Food in Switzerland is on the whole of very good quality. It is also quite outrageously expensive. The reasons for this have to do with high labour costs, high overheads, high land

A variety of breads on sale. Food in Switzerland is generally of good quality, but expensive, due to the high labour costs.

Manserspitz mit
Appenzeller-
Mostbröckli

Fr. 3.50

prices, as well as high transport costs. The big suburban supermarkets are the cheapest, and the high turnover ensures that you can count on getting fresh produce most of the time.

The largest Swiss food chain is Migros, almost a national institution, which started out in the early 1930s as a fleet of trucks that went from village to village with low-priced products, enraging the local grocers but quickly establishing themselves as a highly competitive outlet for consumer goods and basic foodstuffs. In 1948, Gottlieb Duttwieler, their founder and director (who was also involved in Swiss politics), opened Switzerland's first supermarket based on the American model. A strict teetotaller and non-smoker, he refused to stock tobacco products and alcoholic beverages in his shops. Being something of a price shark, he undercut known food manufacturers by having his own labels for many products, and priced them 25–33 per cent cheaper. He also had a nasty habit of ordering in bulk from food companies, making them go broke and then buying them for a song to expand his empire.

The Coop supermarket started as a union-based food co-operative, but has become another aggressive capitalistic retailer in the last three decades. They carry brand names, and sell good, inexpensive wines and cigarettes—the latter quite heavily-taxed in Switzerland, though still rather cheaper than in most surrounding countries.

There are also Saturday or mid-week markets in all of Switzerland's towns and cities, where fresh produce is brought in by various fruit and vegetable growers (often cheese stands too) and sold in very pleasant conditions. These allow you to socialise with the vendors, swap recipes and see whether their produce is organic or not. (Incidentally, Switzerland has quite strictly observed 'green labels' for foodstuff and meats grown in ecologically-sound conditions. More on this a little later on.) In the Basel and Geneva regions, these markets often attract French growers with their rich variety of produce, and cheese and sausage makers with their intriguing variety of regional specialities.

SWISS SPECIALITIES

Speaking of sausages and local specialities, Switzerland offers a delightful variety of edibles—often more or less of farm origins—which are well worth trying.

Sausages

The Saint Gallen region is known for its sausages: the rich smoked-pork Schüblig—a tastier, slightly coarser, giant frankfurter—and the truly unforgettable Bratwurst (which has white veal inside) that you will find in most of the bigger shops throughout Switzerland. The latter are delicious fried or grilled, and can be eaten with an onion sauce, potatoes and cooked apples, or just on a bit of bread, German-style, with a dash of mustard or ketchup (this latter a favourite snack at country feasts). The Stumpen is a Basel variant on the above, although my Basel friends would probably hotly deny this, reciting their own myth of its origin.

Other regions have their sausages too. The Saucisson Vaudois, or Saucisse au choux, is basically chopped-up pork with cabbage inside a skin, hung up to cure in a chalet chimney. Unattractive or even slightly obscene to look at,

it is nonetheless a delicious treat on a cold winter evening. You do, however, have to like things a little on the fatty side.

Sauerkraut

Saucisson, smoked pork fillet and bacon are the staple side dishes of the fine institution of Sauerkraut, which has its origins in a region encompassing northern Switzerland, the southern provinces of Germany and the Alsace region of France. Sauerkraut, essentially shredded pickled cabbage in brine, cooked with a dash of white wine and juniper berries, is an acquired taste; it will bring tears to your eyes—either of love or of hate. For me, a winter without a few feeds of Sauerkraut eaten in good company, with all of the trimmings and washed down with a good lager, would be unthinkable. My wife who is a civilised person mashes a bit with her spuds, and does not share my enthusiasm.

Black Pudding

Another unshared enthusiasm of mine might be traced to my Swiss-German origins: black pudding, sliced and lightly fried with rings of onion, served with potatoes and apple sauce. You don't want to know where black pudding comes from— varieties persist in all of the peasant regions of Europe—and the basis is coagulated pig's blood funnelled into the intestine of the same beast. Catalonia and, above all, Majorca boast spectacular varieties. In Switzerland, the local ones are often quite exceptional, and always very healthy, being full of iron. But if you're not enthusiastic, leave them to the connoisseurs!

Swiss Cheese

So, you've heard that Switzerland is where the cheese has holes in it.

First and foremost, there are dozens of varieties of Swiss cheese. The one called 'Swiss cheese' is locally known as Emmental, from its region of origin, the valley of Emmen in the lush green hinterlands of Bern. The holes—a result of bubbles of carbon dioxide formed during maturation being trapped in the cheese paste—are aesthetically pleasing and

Nothing beats the taste of a freshly-grilled sausage over an open fire.

nice to nibble round when you eat a slice or a lump of this excellent cheese. Much of its delicate flavour comes from the fresh and varied grass fed to the spotted Bernese cows that produce the milk. The best Swiss cheeses now sport origin labels, much like fine French wines.

Another Swiss cheese—this one without holes—is Gruyère (from the Gruyère region between Fribourg and Montreux), which is the cheese usually used to make fondues. Compared to Emmental, it has a rather more distinctive flavour and a faint winey undertaste. A leisurely trip to Gruyère is a must on any tour of the French-speaking Swiss regions. The town of Gruyère, set on a mountain spur with a truly awe-inspiring medieval castle topping it, is a lovely and welcoming place. Go in the strawberry season, and taste that lovely fruit with meringues (from Meiringen, a few mountains over) and the unforgettable local whipped cream. Then, to walk off the

A cheese auctioneer at work—selling the wheels to the highest bidders.

calories, a visit to the cheesemakers would be very educational. You will get to see the various stages of cheese production, from the huge copper pots in which the milk is warmed to the cool cellars in which these wheel-sized cheeses are matured to perfection.

Alp Descent

If you are very fortunate, you may be invited to an alp descent, where the cheese is shared out between the farmers, each according to the number of cows he had on the alp that season. It usually takes place in September, when the mountain is grazed out and the nights begin to be too cold for the animals and their keepers. It is interesting to see democracy in its primordial form, as the price for the product is debated by the alp members, and then sealed by a popular vote. There is usually food and drink, a few blasts of the alpenhorn and much delightful singing and yodelling. At the close of day, the queens of the herd are bedecked with flowers between their horns before the whole group of cows—anything from 40 to 200—trails in zig-zag fashion down the mountain path. While the older folk are packed onto trailers pulled by popping little tractors, the young sprint back and forth with hazel twigs to make sure that Lise and Belle don't lose their way.

One commercially available mountain cheese is Raclette, of Valais origin, which is absolutely delicious melted over potatoes or bread, creating a dish of the same name. The Valais is made up of many valleys, each with its own variety of Raclette cheese, some stronger and more pungent, others mild, but all at their best toasted, with a glass of good wine. Raclette producers have also taken out a patent on the name to protect their wares, and their cheeses are now always marked with an origin certificate.

Appenzell in the east produces its own rather smelly cheese which, like the Tilsiters from the neighbouring Saint Gall region, are an acquired taste to put it mildly. Personally I find it a delicious snack on bread under the grill, although when I confided this to an earnest local cheese maker, he looked at me with a mixture of pity and contempt. The Appenzellers are known for their jokes, but an ability to eat their cheese without flinching, at intervals to smoking their tiny pipes, seems to be a point of masculine honour.

Switzerland is not as well-known as France for soft cheeses. One notable exception is the legendary Vacherin Mont d'Or, from the Joux region in the Jura. This little marvel of a

Various alpine cheeses are also made in mountain pastures, but being small in production, they are not always easy to track down, especially outside their region.

cheese comes neatly cased in a round box made of local spruce. (The French have a very similar product, Vacherin du Haut-Doubs, and there is, of course, dispute over whether this cheese is actually Swiss or French.) You can eat it as it is on good bread, or try this recipe of mine. Preheat your oven to about 200°C (392°F), then boil some spuds. Open

Participants in traditional attire add a sense of festivity to cheese auctions.

the crust of the cheese and pour in a dash of vin de paille (a sweet, straw-coloured white wine, also from the Jura) with a tactfully crushed bit of garlic. Let it melt through the cheese before pouring over the cooked potatoes. A dose of this will make you affectionate, sentimental, good and well-fed.

You will often come across some lovely goat's cheeses produced in small quantities in the mountains and sold at village markets. These vary from young soft lumps—delicious with a few herbs and a thread of olive oil or in salads—to more mature little cakes that are nice with dry rough bread and a good glass of wine. Goat's cheese is a particularly healthy form of taking protein on board as it has virtually no cholesterol, and does not provoke certain allergic reactions that the bovine products are occasionally prone to do.

On the further shores of cheese exotica, and for most an acquired taste, is the Schabziger from the central canton of Glarus. It is a hard cheese made from skimmed milk and a local variety of clover, thus giving it a greenish hue and strong smell. It is normally left to mature for at least a year and keeps for long periods of time. True fans of this cheese prefer those which have been aged, like fine wine, as these are harder and especially pungent. The best way to eat this cheese is to grate or scrape a bit off and mix it with some butter (preferably unsalted) before spreading on sourdough bread. Schabziger is known in the US as sapsago.

In your travels you will find little cheese shops in out-of-the-way villages, or signs pointing to a cheese place on some remote mountain route or walking path which will always lead you to some exotic and olfactory delight, and should often allow you to chat with the beast the stuff came from, or at the very least the cheese-maker. Both might offer a linguistic challenge as neither bovines nor mountain rustics are necessarily overly well-versed in human intercourse.

Fondue

The great gastronomic unifier, though, is of course fondue—a hot cheese-and-wine sauce in an earthen pot into which you dip bread using long forks or skewers. Legend has it that a

Making Fondue

This is a very old recipe for traditional Swiss fondue. It takes about 30 minutes in total, with half that time for preparation.

Ingredients

- 300 g (9.6 oz) of Gruyère, shredded
- 100 g (3.2 oz) of Emmental, shredded
- 100 g (3.2 oz) of a stronger cheese, e.g. Vacherin Fribourgeois, Appenzeller, Tilsiter, similarly shredded
  Your local cheese shop or the cheese counter in your supermarket will shred the cheese for you, and they can also advise you on the choice of cheese. Most have a good fondue mixture they'll make up for you.
- 1 tablespoon of corn flour (Maïzena)
- 1 clove of garlic
- 300 ml of white wine (Johannisberg or Vaudois)
- 50 ml of kirsch
- A few drops of lemon juice
- Pepper and grated nutmeg to taste
- A loaf of white or half-white bread, cut into cubes

Method

First prepare the *caquelon*—a wide pot, either enamelled cast-iron or earthen—which comes with a stand and spirit burner. Rub the inside of the pot with the garlic clove. If you like garlic, leave the clove in there. Dash some wine into the pot and start a low heat on a stove. Combine the three cheeses and add them gradually to the pot. Stir with a wooden spatula over a low heat, allowing the cheeses to melt. The ideal is a figure-of-eight movement.

Mix the corn flour and kirsch in a small cup and add this gradually to the mixture. Keep stirring until the mixture has the appearance of a light, creamy sauce. This normally takes about 5–10 minutes at the most.

Remove the pot from the stove and place over a lighted alcohol safety burner on the table. (Nowadays, a safety paste is available that helps prevent accidents and fires.) Adjust the burner flame so the fondue continues to bubble gently. Season with pepper and nutmeg. The fondue mixture is now ready to be served.

Cheese for Fondue

There are many regional variants on fondue, and it'll be best to adapt your recipe to the regional cheeses of the place where you stay. The local cheese shop will happily make you up a shredded mix and vary it according to your specifications.

16th-century battle at Kappel near Zug between the Zürich Protestants and the Catholics of Uri and Unterwalden was peaceably resolved when the Catholics brewed a milk fondue, and the Zürich troops came up with the bread which they shared and which everyone dipped into the fondue with their spears.

Today, fondue is washed down with white wine, and the occasional glass of kirsch, a firewater which will dissolve the lumps of cheese that might otherwise form in your insides. Etiquette requires you to kiss the person next to you if you drop a lump of bread off your fork into the *caquelon* (as the earthenware pot is called), so there is always a certain amount of discreet jockeying about who you get to sit with.

The Potato

Potato dishes are important to Switzerland. Raclette, where cheese is melted over boiled potatoes, is an alpine must and also a nice urban meal at home. You can either buy or rent the equipment.

The Swiss-Germans are caricatured as 'roesti-eaters', *roesti* being a fried potato cake which is a very solid (some would say stolid) and certainly very filling meal. There are two schools of thought on *roesti*, a Swiss-German one which starts with cooked tubers, and a Savoyard one you will find in the Lake Geneva region where the potatoes are raw and fried tender in a large cast-iron pan. The former variety can be bought pan-ready in supermarkets and is surprisingly good as a quickly prepared snack.

If you're a bit more health-conscious or vegetarian, you'll find what you like here, too. Dr Bircher did rather more than concoct his famous Birchermüesli here. The German word for health food shop is *Reformhaus*, which promises a reforming of your nasty food habits. In everyday life, you'll find organically grown vegetables in most markets, and some supermarkets—notably the Coop—now have a 'green label' line of products grown either organically or under carefully specified conditions. In another but related register, you can also find products labelled by their origin, and the 'fair trade' movement—which assures a decent return for the growers in far-off countries—has its fine products, coffees, teas and certain fruit, widely distributed. The 'Max Havelaar' label, named after a hero in a Dutch series of stories, is based in Basel and remains a useful reference to those who prefer a decent deal to a United Fruit rip-off.

Fruit

Switzerland has a superb variety of fruits. Apples of all kinds abound in the season, and a visit to the apple-growing regions is always worthwhile in September to pick up a case of your favourites to stock in the cool attic until winter. We have about nine varieties of apples growing in the village 3 km (1.86 miles) away, and know the orchardists personally, so we know what we're buying. In the Zug region, cherries abound in spring, and various varieties of plums, peaches and apricots are also regionally available and appear at the markets in season. The Valais apricot, grown at higher altitudes in the clear sunlight, is legendary for its fine taste; alas, its rather late season and high price causes the growers considerable grief given the competition of cheap southern imports.

In strawberry season, you can stew the fruits with rhubarb if you're so inclined, or eat them fresh with whipped cream and meringue. Meringue—although French authorities will deny this—originates in the early Swiss tourist centre of Meiringen in the deep ravines of which a certain Sherlock Holmes came to grief at the dreaded hand of Dr Moriarty. One hopes that the redoubtable Dr Watson was able to seek comfort in a good meringue and whipped cream after that little squabble.

Cake

Fruit means fruit cakes, and Switzerland is proud of its tradition of open apple, plum and apricot cakes—a bit like sweet pizzas—often with a custard sauce. My Zürichois grandmother used to cook wagon-wheel-sized apple tarts on trays placed directly on the coals of her enormous wood stove.

More delicate cakes include the delicious carrot cake from the Zug region, helped along by a dash of kirsch. The latter is also surprisingly delicious in homeopathic quantities to set off various chocolate dishes. Thankfully, the Swiss do not indulge in chocolate fondue.

Birchermüesli

A popular breakfast dish around the world, this is named after the redoubtable Swiss nutritionist, Dr Maximilian Bircher Benner, who was active at the beginning of the 20th century. He had a revolutionary spirit and was one of the founders of Rohkost, or uncooked vegetarian food. The pure and primordial version of this, as stated on the Bircher Sanatorium's website, consists of oatmeal, raw apples, condensed milk, nuts and lemon juice; on this, I was brought up.

In my Swiss-German childhood, we generally ate it not at breakfast but after a light evening meal, with a soup or a salad. There are probably as many versions of muesli as there are people making it around the kitchen. The version I make at home includes rolled oats, shredded coconut, shredded (not powdered) nut, dried raisins, apples, a banana, berries (if available), yoghurt, milk, the juice of half a lemon and a dash of maple syrup.

Roesti

Considered the national dish of Switzerland by some, *roesti* is basically fried grated potatoes. A few cubes of bacon or mushrooms fried with the *roesti* make it delicious; you can also add onions, apples, cheese or fresh herbs. I like to add a finely chopped sprig of rosemary.

The French-Swiss variant of this dish, based on the Savoyard païllason des pommes de terre, starts with *raw* tubers which are then peeled or grated before frying with a little oil and a knob of butter. My son has been known to

add a stirred egg to the mix before cooking, which makes it into a rich and interesting dish.

Papet Vaudois

A dish from the canton of Vaud, bordering Geneva, and one of the many that make winter worth looking forward to. This is purée of leek and potato topped with cheese. It goes well with pork products such as bacon. The Vaudois themselves serve it with saucisson (the smoked pork sausage I talked about earlier). Another alternative is to grate a few hundred grammes of Gruyère cheese into the mixture before it hits the oven. A *papet vaudois* served with stewed apples, good bread and either white wine or lager has been known to make hard men turn all soft and sentimental.

Zürcher Chopped Liver

A fine dish of chopped veal liver, which you'll find in the little restaurants that line the Limmat River, in the centre of Zürich's Niederdorf quarter. It is usually served with *roesti*, but occasionally you'll find it served with buttered egg noodles. Try it with a glass or two of fresh red wine, or a local Riesling Sylvaner.

Gschnätzlets/Geschnetzeltes

Gschnätzlets (try pronouncing this!) is similar to chopped liver but this uses chopped bits of veal escalope instead. It can also be made with chicken or turkey. A dash of cream or cognac (or both, in some cases) may be added at the end of the cooking. Some cooks also add a bit of finely chopped parsley and grated lemon rind on top just before serving.

Polenta

This is a dish from Ticino/Tessin that seems to be known throughout Switzerland. Polenta is a kind of porridge based on cornmeal that has been ground to a kind of semolina consistency. For a long time it was the staple food of the poorer Tessinois and northern Italians—and it is indeed very nourishing. Polenta may be served with a gravy-based dish such as stewed rabbit, or with *ratatouille*—a vegetable casserole, usually made with aubergines—and a crisp green salad.

Risotto

Another filling dish the Tessin shares with the Lombardy region of Italy is risotto. The rice used is usually the variety from the Arborio region, or the 'sticky' short-grain Vialone variety. Risotto is often eaten as a meal on its own. It's also rather nice with breadcrumbed medallions of veal or pork and a fresh green salad.

Gugelhupf

My Swiss-German mother often made this when we had guests on Sundays. Gugelhupf is a light, delicate yeast cake that comes in a distinctive ring shape with lateral flutings, and often filled with candied fruits, raisins and nuts. Some people say it's Austrian (maybe it is), but to me, it looks a bit like the Matterhorn.

A variant of this is marmorkuchen. This tender, buttery cake is based on the marble gugelhupf sold at Demel in Vienna; particularly delicious with coffee on Sunday afternoons.

WHAT DO THE SWISS DRINK?

Lots of water, first and foremost. Taste what comes out of the tap, or what comes burbling from the village fountain wherever you are, and you will be delighted. In the city of Zürich, tap water is drawn from the lake, while fountain water comes from an ancient network of mountain springs, meticulously maintained, and is marvellously good and cool. Bottled water, with or without bubbles, is also available, with a number of regional sources in the western and eastern hills. Valser, Passugger and Henniez are well-known mineral water springs.

A Refreshing Drink

Much of Switzerland's drinking water is quite exceptional in its freshness, purity and taste. I once had an assignment photographing civil engineering installations in the mountainous region of the Valais. I never had to buy a drink. Water sprang everywhere—little burbling stone fountains on village squares, wooden pipes spurdling into hollow logs under clumps of mountain firs, or simply plastic hoses dribbling into bathtubs in the corners of cow-fields. I had a plastic bottle to fill if I wanted to, but ended up mostly slurping from the pipes like a happy bovine.

Wine

Swiss wines, at their very best, are sublime—though some of the regional drops may be acquired tastes. You don't see much of them outside of Switzerland as the harvests are too small to justify a major export market. My wife and I were lucky to be living in the heart of one of Switzerland's largest wine-growing regions—the Mandement, west of Geneva towards the French border—and the wines we drank often came from people we knew pretty well. Many are derivatives of the classic Beaujolais grapes (the Gamay) or of the Pinots that build up Burgundies. Nowadays, many are assemblages, blends of different grapes that often give unique and rounded flavours. One of the whites we enjoy is the Chasselas made from the sugary, tender-skinned, white eating grape which picks up flavours from the ground it's grown in. The locals press them on the slopes with mobile presses to get the first freshness from them and the wine is very good young with slightly sparkly drops. Italian Pinot Grigio, the Burgundy white Aligote and other varieties like Chardonnay are also produced.

Moving around Lake Geneva, the Vaud and Valais have a lot of quite remarkable if sometimes slightly acidic whites that go well with the lake fish. The neighbouring region of Neuchâtel also has some outstanding whites and rosés using the Pinot grape, with some unforgettable stuff from the Auvernier region.

Then there are some rather superb wines to be found in the far east of the country (Grisons) like the legendary and venerable Veltliner. Others are not far from the best Austrian reds. In the Italian region, the staple grape is the Merlot, although there too, there has been a great deal of experimentation by younger winemakers with other varieties and blends.

The wines of the Schaffhausen, Zürich and Thurgau region show more in common with some of the German wines. Many of them are, as I mentioned, a locally acquired taste but try them, by all means, if you happen to be at a table there.

Yodelling

Yodelling sounds utterly wrong in some tourist trap; it must be heard in the mountains. There it can be quite beautiful, almost Baroque in its harmonies, especially when attacked by a bunch of tough blond farmers all in fine falsetto, comfortably stretched out on their backs on a mountain pasture, with a sublime view of the snowy peaks in front of you and a bottle of fresh white wine from the Vaud passing quietly from hand to hand. If you are at such a feast, have a song ready, preferably from your own country. Of course, you can sing!

Beer

Swiss beers are mostly rather like their German or Alsatian cousins, blond and reasonably fresh, with a modest 4–5 per cent alcohol content. Numerous little local breweries have been snaffled up by the big brewers—a worldwide trend, alas—which restricts variety considerably. In the last few years, though, there has been a move throughout the beer regions of Europe and the UK to think small and drink small again. There is a certain amount of interesting concoctions coming out of small breweries that have been taken over by a new generation of younger artisans, like the remarkable little malt brew I tried the other day that's produced in a farming village 15 km (9.32 miles) away.

Ciders

The Thurgau and Bern regions produce various ciders, which you can order at some of the smaller restaurants or buy bottled in some agricultural co-operatives. To my mind, they're not really up to the best Somerset or Normandy Ciders, but again, if you're there, have a taste.

Spirits

The top shelf has not got the variety or renown of our bigger cognac- and grappa-producing neighbours, although the kirsch of Zug is a lovely dessert liqueur and well-known to cooks. Other local products are the Williamine pear brandy, the Zwetschgenwasser plum brandy from the Luzern region, and the Damassine prune brandy from the Jura.

As of March 2005, absinthe became legal again in its country of origin, after a romantic century of bathtub and hillside distilleries producing some pretty toxic firewaters with definite hallucinogenic properties and bad, bad headaches as part of the scenario. If you're into exotic juices, try it. I'm not in a huge hurry myself.

Blood Alcohol Level

Swiss federal law allows a maximum blood alcohol level of 0.5 mg per litre behind the wheel, which represents about a glass and a half to two of wine for an average person. This law is pretty strictly enforced.

Coffee and Tea

If you are a coffee drinker, Switzerland has an excellent variety of fine coffees available from all over the world. Milk coffee is popular at breakfast time, while short Italian-style coffees are drunk in the afternoons. Tea is less of an institution, and unless you're happy with a supermarket teabag in a glass of tepid water, you'll have to shop around a bit more. What you do find is a rich variety of tisanes, from the Linden teas of the Bern canton (almost tasteless and very refreshing) to various concoctions with medicinal or 'mood-altering' properties. My grandmother swore by a hemp-seed tea, which she said kept her calm, and indeed, she was, on the whole, a very calm lady, occasionally known to warble a little.

EATING OUT

Dining etiquette in restaurants is much the same as in other European countries. You can eat as much or as little as you like, but remember your manners, e.g. don't speak with your mouth full. At the end of the meal, the host normally pays. If someone has invited you for a meal and you would like to pick up the tab, offer to pay for the bill. If you host insists on paying, it would be polite to leave it be and return the favour by taking him or her out for the next meal instead.

DINNER INVITATIONS

Someone's asked you to his or her house for dinner, and you accept. What should you do? Remember, first, that dinner invitations are not common in Switzerland and only extended when the host feels really comfortable in his or her friendship with you. You should view it as a mark of respect for you that they would invite you into their home. At this point, it would also be polite for you to mention any food allergies or other dietary restrictions you might have (e.g. if you are a vegetarian or a Muslim). You wouldn't want your hosts to go through a lot of trouble to prepare a meal that you might not be able to ingest.

Going Dutch

In some places and with certain individuals, the restaurant bill is shared at the end—unless someone has formally invited you or it is obvious from the start that someone will be paying for the entire amount. A monthly dinner I attend with a committee in the city works like that: we get a collective bill, do a head-count and pass the hat around. No one is going to worry (within reason) that Marcel had a simple plate of spaghetti, while Catherine had the fillet of salmon, or that old Denis, who has a sweet tooth, finished up with a caramel pudding. What was important was to enjoy the meal and have a good lively discussion together.

It is possible to ask for separate bills of course, but the waiter won't like it, and it can lead to endless calculations about the comparative price of a bottle of bubbly water for Julie and the shares of a carafe of wine that three other guests partook of.

We once had an embarrassing time with the parents of friends of ours on a mountain walk, when they invited us to have a drink and a slice of pie in a small café enroute. We insisted on paying our share, and it was obvious that our principled stand was resented, with the father clamming up and being very distant from then on. Not worth it for 20, 30 francs.

As the Swiss are such sticklers for punctuality, make sure you turn up on time—not early and not late, but on time. If, for some reason, you are held up, be sure to call ahead. This is just being courteous and considerate.

If you come by car, don't park in any of the numbered parking places in front of the housing block. That can cause endless fights and strife. Most apartment houses have 'visitor' car spaces so use these. Otherwise try to find a public spot nearby.

A small gift is always appreciated. This could take the form of a bunch of flowers, a box of chocolates or a bottle of wine. Keep in mind, though, that what is appreciated in one region may not be so in another. For example, some flowers (e.g. red roses, white lilies, chrysanthemums) should be avoided as they carry certain connotations—connotations which occasionally caused raised eyebrows when this author attempted to be courteous. Ask your oldest female work colleague; she would know these things. Sharp objects (e.g. a set of knives or cutlery) are best avoided, as they could be taken to symbolise a cutting of ties between you and the host. Sometimes, even a bottle of wine is not appropriate e.g. in the south (where most Swiss wines are produced) or if your hosts are Muslims. When in doubt, ask other Swiss friends or colleagues for advice. If you can think of some little treat from your corner of the world, that would be ideal. But don't overdo it. Keep things simple and pleasant; if you're out to impress, it could well backfire.

If it's your first time to a dinner and there are other guests present, a round of introductions will be in order, complete with the required handshakes. In more relaxed social settings, first names would be used instead of the usual norm of title and surname. Take your cue from those around you. Remember that it is polite to stand when someone is being introduced to you or you are being introduced to someone. If it's an international gathering, it's likely that language might come into play, so extra effort will have to be made on your part. Feel your way around until you find some common linguistic ground.

A Typical Meal

The Swiss meal pattern is normally a cold entrée or a soup, a main plate and some kind of dessert, cake or fruit as an after. Coffee or tea is usually served after the meal, occasionally with a little glass from the top shelf.

Remember your road safety and, as a related factor, Switzerland's strict drink-and-drive laws.

Food is not a religion in Switzerland, you can eat up what you are served, accept second helpings if you feel like it, or leave a little if it's too much or not to your taste. Drink generally follows a similar pattern, and you should be given a choice between wine and non-alcoholic drinks.

Finally, do not overstay your welcome—remember this is a nation of watchmakers and everything runs according to a schedule. You might like to consider sending your hosts a thank-you note (either a handwritten note or an email) the next day. It is not expected but will be much appreciated. And when you're ready for it, send out dinner invitations of your own, to those who have extended their hospitality and generously opened their homes to you.

ENJOYING SWITZERLAND

CHAPTER 7

"The circus is in town."
—Bob Dylan

GETTING SOME AIR

The Swiss are out a lot. The fact that most of them live in apartments means that their leisure activities often take them away from home, be it for sports or just for outings.

The simplest thing, which is a year-round activity, is to go out for a walk. Wherever you live in this country, you'll have a pleasant venue, or several, near your home. We have three picturesque villages within walking distance, two of which have medieval castles, and a huge natural reserve stretching many kilometres up a stream. In the autumn, a simple walk through the vineyards, occasionally tasting a grape or two, is delightful. (But please don't pick bunches of grapes before the grape pickers have been through. It used to be punishable by death, and is still considered pretty gross.)

Town friends take walks in parks near their homes. You will see lovers and groups of young people sprawled on the grass, folks with small children on the elaborate playground structures and others quietly sitting on benches or under trees asleep with an open book on their lap. Someone might have a dog chasing after a stick on the big patch of grass (dogs should be on a leash, but in some parks, there is a degree of tolerance), while some other people are throwing a frisbee back and forth in the distance. By the lakeside, a family comes by on bicycles on the combined walking and cycle path—mum and dad staid on their brightly-coloured high-tech machines with a baby in the seat attached behind,

while big sister is darting back and forth on her first two-wheeler. On the lake, you can rent rowing boats and pedalos.

So Sundays drift by quietly and pleasantly. There are obviously the usual amenities to make life even more enjoyable. In summer, there are many lake beaches and swimming baths where you can spend happy hours splashing about, picking up a suntan or doing earnest lengths of butterfly crawl. Most indoor pools—usually run by municipalities, and often very beautiful—are open the year round. Lakeside beaches are usually controlled these days by the public health people, and any risk of water pollution (which would be an accident rather than a normal situation) is clearly signalled. Clothing codes are pretty relaxed; you will see many bare breasts, and might like to expose your own if you are so equipped. In most public pools, you'll put tops back on before going into the water. You will be able to work out the dress code of any public swimming place within seconds of arriving. No one is going to come and stare at you, and I trust, gentlemen readers, you will enjoy the pleasant view without making creeps of yourselves.

A local dressed for mountain walking—a popular activity among the Swiss.

A family enjoys a quiet walk in the countryside.

Jass: Favourite Card Game of the Swiss

Throughout Switzerland, regardless of language, Jass is the favourite card game. It is related to the French game of Belote, the English Euchre or 500, and even to bridge.

The game takes 36 standard playing cards, discarding the values below six, and is generally played with four players organised as two opposing teams. Trump is named in turn, depending on the strength of your hand, and you can pass the privilege to your partner if your hand is no good. A poker-like declaring of suits follows.

The hierarchy is rather strange. In normal suits, we start from the ace and go down; in trumps, however, the knave is the strongest (and most valuable) card followed by the nine (called 'Nell'), then the ace, king and queen.

Tricks are played out and the strongest cards dominate, with trumps entitled to cut in over high cards in other suits. Points are counted and carefully noted on a slate, and the game goes on, usually to 1,000 or 1,500 points.

Got that? It may sound confusing to a non-player but there is much to be enjoyed. The game is a very satisfying mixture of skill and luck, and an excellent way to pass a quiet evening.

Don't play with my grandmother though. A mild and very lovely lady, she would became a cruel and heartless harpy at the card table, treating any partner who was not up to scratch to a tongue-lashing which would leave the sensory areas scarred and the mind frazzled. Her brain became a ruthless calculating machine and she could work out precisely who was hoarding the trump card or the ten that she required for her scheme, which was to trounce the rest of us, and go off peacefully to bed as the winner of a glorious tournament.

Did I mention she passed away in 1969? But somewhere in the great beyond, I'm pretty sure she's still gleefully giving them hell.

City folk will also happily catch a train to go for walks or bicycle rides in the country. There are some quite ambitious day trips if you're fit enough, or want to get into physical shape. A retired colleague of mine occasionally puts me to shame by recounting his Sunday cycle tours—90 km (55.9 miles), and 900 m (2952 feet) of climb, seem to be his norm. I might start too when I retire, though it seems a little unlikely. In common with other Europeans, Swiss dress up in cute little cycling suits with tight shorts and brightly coloured sweatshirts as they ride their expensive mounts along sinuous and picturesque routes.

For walking in the country, you will again find many route maps (apart from Switzerland's beautiful 1:25,000 topographical maps), with suggested routes laid out in terms of the time you will take and their difficulty. (I mention a few of these guides and sites in the Further Reading section.) Here, you'd be well advised to have decent, comfortable footwear, an extra layer of clothing (especially at higher altitudes), and a light raincoat with you in one of those nifty little rucksacks all Swiss seem to be born with. If you take a picnic lunch along, you'll probably find good water on the way somewhere or a place where you can buy a drink on a terrace.

The Mountains

Many, many walks are also laid out in the mountains, clearly signposted with generous time estimates to the next place. There also you can often do good trips with public transport links at either end. But you must have appropriate shoes—preferably ankle-high lace-up walking boots with sturdy soles—and you'd be well advised to go with a few friends. More fun, and just a bit more reassuring if someone runs into a spot of trouble such as spraining an ankle.

Don't climb mountains! You've no idea what mountaineering entails and only fools try to walk up the Matterhorn or cross a glacier without an experienced guide.

> Mountains—by their height, by the uncertainty of the weather, and by the foolhardiness of other climbers—are killers.

However, if you have experience in mountaineering, you can obviously ignore my warning. But you will then have enough sense to join ventures with more experienced people, to take a guide or to work through one of the mountaineering clubs attached to universities or larger institutions. The national organisation is the highly respected Swiss Alpine Club, which has representations in most centres.

In any mountain area, you will have access to mountain guides who will be pleased to propose outings, either in groups or individually (more pricey, of course). Few experiences match the beauty and the comradeship of a high mountain trip, but it is a world apart, restricted to those who are up to it.

Snow Sports

What everyone does, naturally, is ski or snowboard. There, again, you'll have to look around to see what your region has to offer, and you'll certainly find places that are accessible without necessarily being lumbered with your car; trains and coaches will get you to many major fields. Again, you'll find propositions of group outings on the notice boards or sites of the organisations or institutions you're attached to.

If you're a beginner, act like one. There is no problem with that and you can learn to ski passably well even at quite an advanced age. Snow sports need to be learned, though with modern equipment most of them are pretty straightforward.

There are essentially three groups, depending on the degree of difficulty of the acitivity. Many people (your writer included) are often happy just to strap on a pair of snowshoes or rackets and to set out on contour walks with a picnic in a backpack plus a well-defined and manageable route set out before you start. It's also a nice way to walk the dog who doesn't bother with snowshoes but leapfrogs over the stuff, leaving flurries as he goes, occasionally running off when he sniffs something.

A slightly more difficult level would be ski walking, where you clip on lightweight skis with long poles suitable for walks up and down the gentle slopes of the Alps, through forests and past beautiful views. This is a fabulous source of fitness, and also gives you some idea of how to handle boards on your feet. Sometimes you have to go down little slopes, where angels hold you upright on strings. Or not—occasionally you land up sitting down. There are no noisy clattering ski lifts and endless cues—a nice sport for the quiet, ecologically-minded people. Costs are also minimal—you can hire the equipment in a sports store, and access to fields is usually free of charge, unless elaborate work has been done for your security and comfort.

If you're into speed and spectacle, you'll want to ski of course. Equipment costs rather more (again, it's best to hire for the first season, to see what kind of gear you're most at ease with) and you'll have to pay a day fee for access to the various lifts, cable cars and other things that get you up to the slopes. In most ski fields, you'll have different prices for different levels, and you'll be well advised to try the beginner slopes initially.

Either you'll be with friends who have enough experience to teach you the rudiments or you'll join a group for a few classes. You should be able to find an instructor who'll speak a language you understand. Learning to ski is enormous fun, and you'll slowly become merely scared rather than utterly terrified as you see little pine trees stretching out their arms in the snow to catch you as you head for them. You will learn how to use a ski lift bar without clattering off into the rockery, how to stop, perhaps how to go around corners, to zigzag to slow yourself down on more hair-raising slopes, and you'll be advised not to cross your skis.

To avoid crossing their skis, some people use snowboards, where both feet are attached to one board. They're rather more difficult to get started on (as far as I know; I'm too chicken to try) but once you are moving on them, they're utterly spectacular. People on snowboards dressed in ghetto-smart style seem to impress the ladies (though many of them are ladies who impress the lads). However snowboards can be very dangerous when the skiers are not quite as much in control as they think they are. One of the things you can do on snowboards is to slither off the tracks onto the steeper looser

Colour-coded Slopes

Swiss ski slopes are coded according to difficulty—from green (easy, grass) to blue (bruises), to red (blood or bloody difficult), to black (it's your funeral).

snow, a practice which provokes a number of avalanches every season which occasionally kill people below them.

As I wrote earlier, mountains are killers, or rather people who abuse them are. So show a healthy respect for the unique and beautiful place you are in.

Snow is, of course, magical for children, and you'll find the temptation to make a snowman with a funny hat and a carrot nose irresistible. Soon, very soon, your little blighters will be screaming past you on their skis or snowboards spraying powdery snow at you and making snide comments about the way you stick out your bum as you zigzag laboriously down a gentle slope waving your ski poles like some freshly sprayed insect.

And the kids will pirate your dwindling purse for hot chocolate and pancakes. Enjoy.

Benjamin's Perfect Day

My cousin Ben came to visit us from New Zealand for a few days, and perhaps get a little skiing. Luck was with him as our elder son, an experienced mountain skier, was on holiday from university. He and his girlfriend Julia were happy to take Ben—who was already quite good on his board—in hand for a few days. They had a nice place in the mountains they could use, thanks to Julia's dad; so they pinched our elderly family car, suitably shod with snow tyres, with a pair of tyre chains thrown in the back, and set off.

In Villars, they met up with a pal of theirs working there as a ski instructor and mountain guide. Villars, in the Vaud Alps, is one of those skiing places where a little red train emerges from a tunnel and whistles to a halt in the snowfields, with ski lifts clattering all around, and the happy scraping of skiers and snowboarders in brightly coloured anoraks coming to a stop next to the little station.

They warmed up on blue tracks, graduated to red, and beetled down a black track during the quiet part of the day. They saw an avalanche (a little one) bucketing down a gully and learnt which areas to avoid so as not to set off, or get caught by, these murderous snow attacks.

Lunch was bread and cheese with a glass of beer in the sun, looking across the valley at the majestic French Alps capped by Mont Blanc.

When they left at the end of the day, they piled into the car and went to a nearby thermal watering place in Lavey, where a warm dip and sauna relaxed their juddered muscles and put them into the sweetness of humour one loves of alpine evenings. Followed a visit to a cosy restaurant—with wood panelling, chintz curtains and lampshades—where honour was done to a fondue and a bottle of local white wine. Vineyards were visible under the snow across the valley, with a huge medieval castle cradled in the middle. Then it was back to Papa's chalet for a good mug of hot tea and a few rounds of Jass with a vigilant partner. And then to bed.

Sports

If you're into organised sport, you'll find many clubs in the country and facilities for most sports you might like to play. At the village here, we play pétanque, a kind of bowls game from France involving steel balls and a little wooden marker called the *cochonnet* or 'piglet'.

A traditional Swiss sport, found in some alpine regions, is Hornussen (or 'Hornets') where a small, hard rubber ball is whipped into the landscape to a range of about 300 metres (328 yards), and the opposing team throws wooden panels (a bit like barn doors) into the air to try to intercept the 'hornet'. These guys could wreak havoc on a golf course destroying birdies in mid-flight. And why is the game called Hornussen? The whizzing sound that ball makes as it travels through the air at about 300 km/h (186 mph) is much like that of a hornet, hence the name.

Most towns and many villages have tennis courts. Understandably, the Swiss are rather good at tennis internationally. Shop around a little; clubs can be rather expensive but most places have municipal facilities. You won't find municipal golf courses though, or polo grounds, so be prepared to pay, unless your workplace provides access to some facility. Sailing, too, will probably belong to more of an elite world than where you come from, and moorings for keelers on the lake change hands at the price of luxury cars. Curling clubs flourish in the cold season. For the young and more agile people, surf-skiing is a major summer sport and Swiss lakes are enlivened by pretty Delta sails darting along with the breeze.

Parapente, or jumping off mountains while dangling from parachute gliders, is a pretty big thing here too, and many high places keep their cable cars running in summer. The sky then fills up with little coloured specks floating on the thermals like thistledown.

Most team sports will cost you the price of a club annual membership fee. Football is a national sport here, with countless clubs based on regions or on origins—there is a very good Arab club in Geneva, a ferocious Albanian club, a friendly but efficient Portuguese club and several Italian clubs—and different levels of amateur leagues. All of the other ball games—rugby, handball, volleyball, basketball,

Some people like bungee jumping, it seems. There is no shortage of high places here, and lots of elastic.

etc—are around, and evenings are active with enthusiastic games in village halls and sports centres. Rather than listing them all, I would say that every imaginable sport has its club in most main centres, and the main centres are never far away from wherever you might be living. Any place you move to will gladly give you a list of local clubs and facilities.

ART AND CULTURE

At a regional and local level, Switzerland is very much alive culturally. All walks of life have access to various aspects of the artistic and cultural movements and traditions that are vital for the spiritual and mental health as well as the balance of any population.

On the national level, there are a number of centres that monitor and encourage art and culture, and they are involved in subsidising individual creators or institutions, such as theatres and museums, that transcend national boundaries. The most important foundation, Pro Helvetia, is technically an NGO under government supervision which helps dispense cultural subsidies to the tune of about 30 million francs a year. They are quite happy to enter into polemics, as they did in 2004 when there was an attempt to muzzle an artist who had done some (not very brilliant) satirical work on one of the coarser members of the Swiss cabinet.

On the ground, you will see a cultural budget under the aegis of the education ministries of most cantons, and a cultural service attached to most towns and cities.

Cultural Involvement

Get involved culturally too, if that's your thing. Drama groups, operatic societies (including one in Geneva that specialises in American and English musical comedy), choirs, orchestras, bands, literary groups, art societies, church groups, etc—the range is endless and you'll find a good welcome there if you're prepared to do your part. Moving to a new country entails making contacts which can ripen into friendships, and the opportunities are as rich here as anywhere else in the world.

For you, this means that you will be able to attend a pretty good variety of cultural events at all levels, usually at reasonable entry prices.

The Musical Arena

If you like classical music, Switzerland boasts a number of fine regional orchestras, of which the Tonhalle Orchestra in Zürich and the Orchestre de la Suisse Romande in Geneva are the best known. The Lugano-based Orchestra della Svizzera Italiana seems to be very much in demand for tours and recordings, and Lausanne has a fine chamber orchestra which, under Christian Zacharias, has done some beautiful Mozart in the last few years, while also tackling the 20th century repertoire for smaller formations.

In Zürich and Geneva, the orchestras are also active in the two Swiss opera houses that are part of the European circuit: the Zürich Opernhaus and the Grand Théâtre de Genève. These offer a rich and varied season. There are also productions in Bern, Basel, Lugano and Luzern, not to mention the yearly open-air production at Avenches. Ballet forms part of their programmes, and the bigger centres have dance companies attached to them. Maurice Béjart's dance ensemble has put Lausanne on the map as a centre of excellence in imaginative modern ballet. The big opera houses are not always easy to get into, and if your workplace has a ticket offer, jump to it. We have occasionally been able to go to dress rehearsals through the university or the polytechnic; but for the Béjart *Don Giovanni* a few years ago, I spent a day queuing outside the Grand Théâtre with the sharp-elbowed, fur-coated brigade.

Most cities have their concert season, with local and invited orchestras as well as resident and invited conductors and soloists. There seem to be recitals and chamber music concerts in every village with more than three houses and two cows. In the small village where we live, a Baroque series had guest performers of the quality of Gustaf Leonhart on a harpsichord in the local castle.

In terms of jazz and pop events, Switzerland is also amply and beautifully covered, with regular concerts by international names and countless concerts by local musicians. Many of the most pleasant events take place in summer, when mystical places like Engelberg in the Bernese Oberland form lovely backdrops for the decibels

A Hungarian trio entertains on the street.

of local artists like Stephan Eicher. But in winter, too, you'll find many city venues—from dusty old concert halls or converted industrial spaces to the grubby cellars of squats—offering surprisingly good stuff.

Visual Arts

As befits a country as wealthy as Switzerland, you will find some fine art museums here, with staggering permanent collections, and exciting, mind-expanding shows.

It is impossible to describe every centre so let's take Basel as an example. Outside of the city, in Riehen, is the Beyeler Foundation—a beautiful building designed by Renzo Piano—which not only has one of the finest 20th-century private collections in Europe but also holds a superb annual exhibition. In the city, the Kunstmuseum is a world centre for contemporary art, and also houses some fine Renaissance material, of which the Holbeins are the best known. The Kunsthalle is another museum—with a more pedagogical and documentary function. The city also boasts an exciting museum which houses its collection of Jean Tinguely works—his mad clattering machines and rattling metaphysical mysteries, completed by a fountain by the same artist near the cathedral. Modern architecture has a small but indispensable museum in the city centre devoted to it. Add to this countless dealer galleries, which deal in everything from Russian icons and African masks to last week's video performance by some cutting-edge newcomer, and you'll get some idea of the scope of the place. An annual art fair, Art Basel, in June, has been described as 'the most significant international annual fair of contemporary art'.

A similar picture can be drawn of most major Swiss cities, although you will find specialised collections in less important

centres. So, in the field of photography, for example, there are two major museums—one in the industrial city of Winterthur, half an hour outside of Zürich; the other in the Elysée, Lausanne, just above the Olympic museum, with a view on the lake.

If you like stained glass, go to any of Switzerland's fine churches that have escaped the ravages of the 20th-century wars (although in some cases the Protestant mobs did the damage four centuries earlier) or to the very fine specialised museum in Romont.

The field of anthropology has an international museum attached to the University of Neuchâtel, known for its thought-provoking annual exhibitions dealing with the fundamental questions of our existence.

The art of the insane has the fascinating Art Brut Museum in Lausanne; food has its museum in Vevey (with a giant fork stuck in the lake in front of it); and watches have a number, including two in Geneva.

Living museums

Of course, most Swiss towns are museums in themselves. The Zytgloggeturm in Bern is a marvel of Renaissance clockwork technology, the Munot fortifications outside Schaffhausen are awesome in their size, and the mysterious castle of Chillon is just one of dozens that are well worth a visit. The traditional Swiss country house—in its many regional variants—has a beautiful open-air museum dedicated to it in Ballenberg, in the Interlaken region east of Bern.

SWISS FEASTS

A calendar of all the feasts in Switzerland would be a pretty hefty volume—every little locality seems to have its own ritual of fountain dipping, burning the snowman or running the village street with cowbells. Some of these feasts go back to antiquity, many are religious in origin, while others just seem to have sprung up for no very good reason. Wherever you are in Switzerland, you will quickly pick up on what is being done locally—so enjoy!

HOLIDAYS

Although each region and canton has its individual holidays, the following are legal holidays all around the country:

- New Year's Day (Neujahr/Jour de l'an/Capodanno): 1 January
- Good Friday (Karfreitag/Vendredi Saint/Venerdì Santo): Usually in late March, the first Sunday after the first full moon after the Spring Equinox
- Easter Sunday and Monday (Ostern/Pâques/Pasqua): Second and third day after Good Friday
- Ascension Day (Auffahrt/Ascension/Ascensione): Forty days after Easter Sunday
- Whit Sunday and Monday (Pfingsten/Pentecôte/Pentecoste): Tenth and eleventh days after Ascension Day
- National Day (Bundesfeier/Fête nationale/Festa nazionale): 1 August (celebrates the Oath of 1291, which is considered the start of the Swiss Confederation)
- Federal Fast (Bettag/Jeûne fédéral/Digiuno federale): Monday after third Sunday of September, except in Geneva where the Genevan Fast is celebrated on the Thursday after the first Sunday of September. As strange as it may sound, these two days are actually *feast* days and not days for fasting.
- Christmas Day (Weihnachten/Noël/Natale): 25 December

January to April

New Year has a number of odd local ceremonies attached to it, of which the most magnificent is the Sylvesterchläuse in the Appenzell region. It is essentially composed of men with amazingly fine rococo women's masks, accompanied by others dressed as trees, who do a kind of extended pub crawl up and down the snowy valleys with torches, lustily singing songs and behaving in a somewhat bawdy manner, imbibing whatever is available through straws so as not to have to remove their masks. The origins of this extravaganza must go back to the dawn of pagan times. There is a second feast on Saint Sylvester Day, 13 January, as Appenzell was rather slow at going from the Julian to the Gregorian calendar. Anyway two feasts are better than one!

Carnival

Carnival—celebrated just before or just after the start of Lent, depending on the canton—is a big event with countless varieties of feasting throughout Switzerland. As befits a slightly puritan culture which nevertheless loves to enjoy itself, the variety of rituals dances and masks would fill a book on their own. Again, wherever in Switzerland, keep a lookout from about mid-January to mid-February and there's bound to be something exotic or amusing going on in your town or your region.

In the Lötschental valley (Valais), there is the tradition of masked men marauding about at this time of year. The masks, which are designed to be scary and grotesque, are truly amazing, often made from gnarled local wood coarsely carved to resemble faces, and worn with the grubbiest sacking goatskins and other odd clothing. The feast is quite anarchic, and it seems that both church and state have, in their time, tried to suppress or calm it. An Internet site (http://swissworld.org) concludes laconically: "However, the monsters have given up the practice of spraying young girls with manure and emptying sacks of ashes over them." I suppose that could be seen as progress.

But the largest and most spectacular carnival by far is in Basel, where the feast reaches Venetian proportions while keeping a unique and local flavour that goes with that fine city. It takes place over four days in the week after Ash Wednesday, beginning with a Morgenstreich (a type of march) played an hour before dawn when groups of fifes and drums suddenly appear in the streets of the old town and start marching as they play. Few things are more thrilling than the sound of pipes and drums against stone walls in the cold morning air. Later in the day, a cortège is formed with endless masks, floats and satirical broadsheets or Schnitzelbanks usually ferociously satirising local issues (this is an allusion to the fine tradition of Basel's

Other cities—notably Lucerne, and more recently Bern and Onex in Geneva—also organise huge Carnivals. These play on local issues or, in the case of Onex, multi-ethnicity, with the local Brazilian population taking the lead. However, Basel still remains the reference.

free printers' guilds which date back to Gutenberg) as well as the noisy music of Guggemusik, a lovely 20th-century Swiss adaptation of the Rio Carnival's exuberant music, using everything from garden hoses and washboards to well-worn brass instruments.

Easter

The celebration of Easter coincides with the regeneration of the seasons and this leads to many feasts—some religious, other rather pagan. For a Christian experience, the Easter night singing in the Russian churches in centres that have them (like Geneva) is unforgettable. On Good Friday in Romont, in the Catholic canton of Fribourg, there are the crying women, the Pleureuses, who were initially part of a mystery play, and who follow a symbolic cross through the streets, weeping and wailing.

Easter is a boon to Switzerland's many chocolatiers, who make splendid filled-eggs in chocolate and nougat, as well as glorious chocolate Easter bunnies. Dairies make lambs and rabbits in butter. Families sit around the kitchen table decorating hard-boiled eggs with inks and paints. Some of the prettiest traditional ones use solutions of onion skin or certain woods with fronds of leaves tied to the eggs as they are boiled. This gives them delicate filigree patterns over natural brown and ochre colours. Traditionally, eggs (chocolate and real) are hidden, either around the apartment or in the garden, and gleefully hunted out by everyone on Easter morning. At lunchtime, Tütschen is the name of the game, as eggs are cracked against each other and the strongest wins.

The Nyon Porcelain Museum on Lake Geneva puts the finest eggs on show every year, with the Russian community coming in with some exquisite examples which would make Fabergé blush. The Swiss-Germans throw them. Yes, in Frümsen in the Appenzell Säntis region and in a few other places, the village people gather on Easter Monday on a large sloping meadow; decorated eggs—boiled rock hard—are lustily thrown downfield, with the egg throwers suitably turned out in fancy dress. There is a prize for the egg that is thrown the furthest, without breaking, of course. If you have

a background as a cricket fielder, you might like to try out for this competition.

May/June

Early summer brings people and their animals outdoors. I've described the annual bull/cow fight in the Herens region of the Valais in Chapter 3, where the Alp herds fight out which beast is to be their leader. This usually happens sometime in May or June, when the village farmers decide that conditions are right and off they march with their beasts and their cheese-making gear to a summer in the mountains.

Another feast, quite recent but which has become very important, is the annual Feast of Music, usually held in the last weekend of June when the days are long. This is essentially an open day for musicians in all of Switzerland's main centres, and huge crowds of people throng the concert halls and various open-day venues to take in everything from Rameau to rap, with the usual stands for drinks and various kinds of food to eat as you listen.

Music Festivals

Speaking of music, Switzerland has countless music festivals, some with international impact, others only locally known, but most worth a visit. For popular music, the Nyon Paléo Festival has become a big international event for a mixture of European and international singers. It takes place in early July. Then there is the very important international Jazz Festival in Montreux, usually in the first fortnight of July, for which you must book ahead. Another event you have to book in advance is the most prestigious classical music event, the Lucerne Festival, which is now in two parts, at Easter and in July. It takes place in Switzerland's most beautiful concert hall, a Jean Nouvel creation on the shores of Lake Lucerne. Being such high-profile events, the tickets for these tend to be priced on the high side. A slightly more modestly priced jazz festival takes place in Gurten in Bern, usually in the last fortnight of July. There are countless other summer delights, often the more fun for being a little out of the way.

A local college choir performs during the music festival.

August

The one important national feast is on 1 August—a patriotic occasion commemorating the 1492 oath on the field of Rütli between the three original states of the Swiss Confederation. All Swiss towns and villages celebrate it in the evening. Generally, soup is served to all comers followed by a procession of village children bearing paper lanterns; then a huge bonfire is lit, commemorating the signalling fires used for centuries to warn of incursions and raids. The local band plays, the assembled citizens sing the national anthem (a pretty nice 19th-century hymn) and some dignitary is wheeled up to make a patriotic speech. The evening culminates in a massive show of fireworks, with the local village fire brigade doing the official bit, and the village or town children blasting off with whatever they have managed to buy.

Fire and Rain

One of the most memorable national feasts we attended was in the country one year when there was a very severe drought in July and fireworks were banned. It was a sultry hot evening and as the bonfire sparked up, a rainstorm started. The whole village danced around the flames in a circle, soaking wet and jubilant until late into the night.

August is also the time of two major fireworks nights—one as part of the Fêtes de Genève around the 12th; the other, a little earlier, in the city of Kreuzlingen near Konstanz. Street parades of magnificently garish revellers take place in Geneva and Zürich around those dates as well.

For horse fanciers, the big summer occasion is the annual horse market in the isolated Jura region of Saint-Légier, on the second Sunday of August. The Franches-Montagne region has its own very pretty breed of tough little chestnut horses, and the various races, demonstrations of different carriages and general fun make this an exceptionally pleasing day. The more so as the Jura in August is beautiful, cool, green and clear, and some of Switzerland's finest (though not cheapest) restaurants are in the region.

Locarno Film Fest

Switzerland's most important film festival is held in Locarno, in the second week of August. It allows Swiss filmmakers to showcase their work with the best from all over the world. The films are projected onto a big screen in the charming Swiss-Italian town's main square.

September

A recent annual event in September is the Day of Monuments, usually held on the first Saturday of the month. On this day, a number of important old (or not so old) buildings and installations are open to the public. Everyone is invited to visit these places in the company of guides to gain a better understanding of the architectural and engineering tradition of the country.

September is the season for wine and harvest festivals. The dates vary a little, but they are generally at the weekends. Russin, in the Geneva region, has one in mid-September and this can easily draw a quarter of a million visitors over a weekend. Various groups come in with floats decorated with flowers, through the two streets of the village, which are flanked with tables for food and wine tasting. Neuchâtel, as befits a largish centre, has the same, but on a far bigger scale, as does Vevey on Lake Geneva.

November

November is a time for markets of the summer's produce, the most famous being the great onion market in Bern. Locally called Zibelemärit, this takes place on the last Monday of November. It offers the most amazing collection of onion stands on the town's four main squares—the onions neatly pleated into strings, together with other agricultural produce such as potatoes and cheese. The Bernese get up early for this one—the feast starts at 5:00 am and there are usually ample quantities of freshly baked onion flan on sale for a bracing breakfast in the cold. As with many markets, there is a fun-fair on the side, usually set up near the parliament building. You will find children playing at the shooting galleries or riding on carousel rides and the big wheel well into the night.

Target shooting, usually with military rifles, has a long tradition in some circles in Switzerland (shooting at rifle clubs was long a compulsory part of a citizen's military obligations). On 11 November—the day of the patron saint for hunting, Saint Martin—a huge shooting feast is held on the Rütli field, in the centre of Switzerland, where many targets are punctured and much eating and drinking of traditional Swiss goodies goes on. Every canton's rifle club brings in a seasonal contribution from its region. So even if you can't hit a haystack at a metre with an Uzi, you can still enjoy wagon-wheel-sized onion, cheese and apple flans from the north, roasted chestnuts from the Tessin, or Basel sauerkraut, all washed down with generous quantities of the various Swiss wines and ales.

Goose Festival

One of the weirder autumn feasts is the Gansabhauet or beheading of the goose in the town of Sursee, in the canton of Luzern. This takes place on 11 November and involves caped and gold-masked youths armed with sabres, trying to behead a dead (thank heaven!) goose suspended on a wire in the town square. The winner gets to eat the beast. Obviously not a feast for vegetarians.

December

In many of the northern centres, Saint Nicholas is feasted on the 6 December. This saint is based on the 4th-century figure of Saint Nicholas of Myra, protector of the young. He is often accompanied by a kind of alter ego, Black Peter, Schmutzli or Père Fouettard, whose function is to punish naughty children by lunging after them to beat them with a bundle of sticks, while good Saint Nicholas hands out nuts, chocolates and mandarins to their well-behaved brothers and sisters. I have a memory of one of my little cousins being severely scared by Schmutzli, who threatened to take her away to the dark forest in his big bag for some misdemeanour. She has been good ever since, if a little nervous. Some of the Saint Nicholas outings are extremely colourful, notably in the central and eastern regions of the country, where they go to great lengths in their processions, with elaborate costumes enthusiastically accompanied by church bells and the clanging of every cowbell that can be mustered. Fribourg has a major religious feast in its cathedral on the day, Saint Nicholas being the city's patron saint.

A major December feast in Geneva is the Escalade, which commemorates an attempt in 1602 by the Savoy troops to scale the walls of Geneva—at that time a Protestant and Republican bastion surrounded by hostile Catholic forces on three sides. The legend holds that an old woman, who lived in a house overlooking the city wall, was busy late at night with a large cauldron of vegetable soup when she heard the soldiers clambering up. She gave the alarm by pouring the boiling contents of her cauldron on the heads of the invaders, who were swiftly repulsed by the local garrison. Nowadays, there is a huge parade, with harquebusiers and horsemen in 17th-century costume and armour riding through the town reading a proclamation and singing the Escalade song at various points; this culminates in a dance around a huge cauldron of soup in front of the Saint Pierre Cathedral. The soup is then consumed with great relish, accompanied by warm wine. The local chocolatiers make beautiful cauldrons filled with marzipan fruit which are gleefully smashed in homes or at parties throughout Geneva. Traditionally, the oldest and the youngest member of the gathering smash the pot together, with their linked hands shouting (in French naturally), "So perish the enemies of the republic!"

A small mid-December feast that lives in my memory is Bochselnacht, celebrated in my little native town of Weinfelden in the Thurgau region. Essentially the feast is not unlike Halloween, with a distribution of turnips to schoolchildren who industriously hollow them out, illuminate them from the inside with a candle and put grotesque masks on them. They then carry these turnips through the town in a procession, singing a song about enjoying life while you can. This custom goes back to the Middle Ages where a good percentage of people—among them many children—would not see spring again, being wiped out by diseases of which the plague was only the most spectacular.

Skiing in the Dark

During the ski season, most of Switzerland's many ski centres organise occasions when you can ski off mountains in the darkness, holding pine knot torches as you snake down to the village. Not really for debutantes, I'd say, but you're more than welcome to join the fun at the arrival over a glass of mulled wine or cocoa.

Christmas is a lovely feast throughout Switzerland, where there is often snow on the ground in the higher or more northern regions, and where Christmas markets are held in many town squares, selling simple and pretty presents from all over the world. Most Swiss celebrate Christmas *en famille*, with a decorated tree lit with candles in the living room, and a pleasant couple of days of excess, and peace and joy on earth. Churches tend to have midnight services. The feast tends to be a little more decorous and sober than the American or even English variety—silly hats would not usually find their place, and Father Christmas has long done his rounds by then, having come through on Saint Nicholas Day.

To close this chapter of delights, here are some parting words: look around, admire the posters on hoardings, surf the net. Every year, there are more and more tourist calendars on all of Switzerland's Internet sites and these are an endless mine of cultural and simply fun events.

THE SWISS LANGUAGES

CHAPTER 8

"He could not speak but only chatter."
—Bob Dylan

IN COMMON WITH BELGIUM, another small country, Switzerland has several official languages—primarily for historical reasons. The three languages are Swiss-German, French and Italian. (There are also a few odd eastern mountain valleys where the old generation still converses in various languages grouped as Romansch.) All official documents are, by law, required to be available in the three major national languages. Of the majority language groups, some 74 per cent are Germanic, some 20 per cent French and the rest Italian-speakers.

One Name in Many Languages

A rather sweet story was told to me some time ago. At a motorway rest area, a Swiss gentleman came upon an American couple with a rental car poring over a road map of Switzerland. Being a kindly soul, he asked them in his best schoolboy English if they were needed help.

"Waal yes, we're heading for Lausanne," replied the man.

"No problem," said the Swiss. "About 50 km—that's 30 of your miles—down the road and you'll be there."

"And that's where the wooden bridge is, right?" the gentlemen asked.

The Helvetian scratched his head. The Americans then produced a postcard of the famous wooden bridge in Lucerne.

Continued on next page

Continued from previous page

"Well no, Lucerne is three hours' drive from here. You'd have to be heading the other way..."

The wife chipped in, "Wait a minute, Switzerland's got three languages, right?"

"Yes, but..."

It transpired that our enthusiastic motorists had decided with considerable linguistic imagination that Lausanne was the French name for Lucerne, and that the picturesque Swiss Italian town of Locarno was the Italian name for the same place.

Back in Arkansas, there are some who confuse Switzerland, Sweden and Swaziland, I'm told; may this guide serve them well in Mbabane!

A boundary divides Switzerland irrevocably, as definitely as Germany used to be divided between East and West: the *Röstigraben* for our Swiss-German friends, the *Rideau de Roesti* for the Frenchies. *Rösti* is a stodgy and solid preparation of shredded-and-fried potatoes, considered the staple diet of Swiss-Germans and rather looked down on by French- and Italian-speakers delicately fingering their *frites* (chips) or spooning their *polenta* (maize porridge). This 'border' runs across the country in a roughly north-west line, cutting a swath of the canton of Bern, and using the Saar River as a border in the canton of Fribourg (or Freiburg as it is called in its German-speaking region). The cities of Freiburg and Bienne are as bilingual as Brussels, with most citizens switching from one to the other with disconcerting ease and elegance, although everyone identifies with one or the other language community from their family links and often the part of the town they are from.

For the Swiss-French, Swiss-Germans are a rather peculiar breed and are treated warily as the linguistic and financial majority of a small and not overly cohesive country. They make fun of them, although, in fact, Swiss-Germans are better at making fun of themselves, with some unforgettable comedies and cabaret acts based on their linguistic peculiarities—which are, of course, all but incomprehensible to non-German speakers.

SWISS-GERMAN

Many jokes, generally unkind, have been made about the Swiss-German language.

It is like a very far-removed poor relation of German, a bit like Pidgin English vis-à-vis English, with its own vocabulary adaptations and oddities, and a pronunciation which makes grown men glassy-eyed. George Steiner described it succinctly as a throat disease, and it is, indeed, in most of its forms, spiced with more throat-clearing, hacking and other more or less disgusting sounds than would seem to be strictly necessary.

As becomes the language of a small country, it is also crawling with diminutives. My father-in-law, a calm and composed Dutchman (Dutch is not one of the prettier languages either, I might add, but don't tell Cornelius I said that), gets by on his visits to the northeast by speaking perfect poker-faced Dutch—but adding the suffix -li to every second word (for example, to say 'house', he takes the Dutch *hus*, adds a -li, and gets *hüusli*, which most felicitously is the right Swiss-German word for 'house')—and no one's ever raised an eyebrow. They probably just wonder which region he comes from. The people of most regions will very quickly identify your origin by your accent. My Swiss-German grandmother, who for most of her life was never more than 10 km from her birthplace, would be able to tell you not only which village in our canton (Thurgau) you came from, but also which end of the village, just by monitoring your vowels and inflexions.

Similar to many dialects, Swiss-German is a remnant which followed its own route of development because its speakers were isolated, as much from the main German region as from one another. So if you come across poems and texts in German from the High Middle Ages (that's in the 12th century—come on, there must be at least one reader who studied High German; don't leave me all alone!), they will often look and presumably sound a bit like Rhine Swiss-German. You'll hear pockets of dialect nearly as bizarre as Swiss German in the outer reaches of Bavaria or Styria in Austria, for similar geo-historical reasons.

Oddly, apart from a few poems and popular songs, there

is no written form, as such, for Swiss-German; the language is just too varied to be trapped in writing except in pretty elaborate transcriptions of various dominant dialects. A colleague of mine of Zürich (and Russian!) origin used to correspond with his girlfriend in Zürich dialect. It looked, to put it mildly, very peculiar and seemed on the verge of kinky as an infliction on an otherwise charming girl. Other forms that are common are Bärndütsch, Baseldütsch and Ostdütsch (the rather flat language I grew up with). Swiss-Germans write (and speak with a slightly pompous air) perfectly adequate high German (Schriftdeutsch) for administrative and even literary purposes.

If you happen to speak German, you'll find this useful as a *passepartout*, although in some regions, you'll be looked at as a toffee-nosed foreigner, a bit like sporting a home counties accent in a Glasgow pub. Even between German and Swiss-German, there are many piddling but significant differences. Take those exasperating German genders. The language sports three of them, the '*der, die, das*' business. The Swiss use three too, but many words vary, so *das Butter* in good German becomes *de[r] Butter* to the Swiss. To make matters worse, the word for the spready stuff itself changes in the Bern region to *Anke*. Swiss-German also borrows many words from its French-speaking neighbours. No *danke* ('thanks') for our Swiss, he'll say *merci*, or if he's really grateful, he won't flinch before the bizarre Franco-German mix of *merci vielmal* ('many thanks'). Where his German cousin catches the Strassenbahn in Munich, he'll be just as happy to clamber aboard a tram in Zürich or Basel, like any Genevan, Neuchâtelois or Englishman. If you eat out, you'll ask for the *menu* like a civilised Switzer, and leave the leather-trousered German clamouring for a *Speisekarte*.

Many Swiss-Germans spend a year of their studies in the Swiss-French part, a practice that has the endearing appellation of *Welschlandjahr*. To them, it seems Swiss-French are as much greasy foreigners as the Welsh to the Brits, but that, again is another story. It allows them to learn a civilised language and occasionally to discover the charms of the opposite sex, though they tend to club and group around together, noisily chattering in their own tongue and causing the staid Suisses-Romands (as the Swiss-French call themselves, from an inaccurate historical paradigm which makes the French-speaking region the equivalent of the area occupied by the Romans) to cluck their tongues and look out of the windows of their trams.

SWISS-FRENCH

The French spoken in the Suisse Romande, although it has its variations, is pretty close to the standard Paris product, and can certainly be understood by our Gallic cousins. They have a few oddities, as the Belgians, the West Africans and the French Canadians do, but they are mostly easily decoded. They have, for example, simplified the absurd French system of counting where 95 becomes *quatrevingt-quinze* (in effect 'four twenty fifteen', mad!) and use the rather simpler *nonante-cinq* like the Belgians. The French snigger at them, but they blanch—as do our German friends—when the Swiss coolly use Anglicisms in the place of some of the more absurd constructions they have cooked up to get around using a word dropped on them from perfidious Albion. So we will go away for *le weekend*, to a wellness centre in the Valais, perhaps do a little *footing* (jogging!) and a workout in *le fitness* after we've had our *brunch* or perhaps just *un sandwich*. It'll be nice to relax after a week of *stress* at the office where I suspect *le manager* of mobbing me.

What is important to you, if you are a speaker of English, is that most Swiss (especially Swiss-Germans) will be able to answer you quite adequately in English, which they will have learned for between three and six years if they've been to junior high and college, and which they will often have improved by stays in an English-speaking environment during their training or studies. In fact, according to a recent study, Swiss from different linguistic regions will often prefer to use English over one of the national languages, on the very democratic assumption that it puts both interlocutors on the same language footing. With you, they'll be delighted to use their English, and will be even more pleased if you compliment them on it.

If you come in speaking only Bahasa Indonesia, Swahili, Norwegian or Latvian, you will find others speaking your language in the main cities, which is good news. But in the long run, if you're counting on staying in the country, you'd be wise to make an effort to learn the local languages a little. Swiss will enormously appreciate your efforts in that direction and will do everything they can to encourage you and correct you in your fledgling efforts. Evening courses in Swiss-German conversation are available in most of the region's main centres and, of course, there is a generous and very full offer in French and Italian in those linguistic regions.

Where to Learn the Language

One of the more widespread institutions in the field is attached to the enormous Swiss supermarket chain Migros, and some of the Swiss university-level schools are now recommending these courses for foreign students.

LEARNING THE LANGUAGES

Can you, and should you, learn the local languages ? I suspect the question will depend a little on you, where you come from, how long you plan to stay here and in which linguistic corner you've struck your delicate little roots.

So if you're in from Budapest for a three-month stay in Zürich, forget it. You'll have a bit of German and possibly English from school; make do with those, and amuse the local cheese shop owner by saying a bright *merci vielmal, bis später* ('thank you, see you later') as you walk out. At the end of your stay, assuming you haven't sulked in your room all that time, you will suddenly be surprised at how much you have picked up.

But if you're Anglophone (yes that's what they call English-speakers here) and you end up in Geneva, you'll be learning or perfecting your French. The big difference is that French is an internationally accepted language whereas Swiss-German remains a somewhat eccentric dialect. What's more, English and French are linguistic cousins, so you'll find a lot

of your vocabulary already laid on if you take a bit of time and possibly a few basic lessons. You can be sure that you'll be very much appreciated if you make the effort, and that even if people smile at your occasional mistakes, they won't laugh at them.

You will find getting about pretty straightforward. The fact that Switzerland is a trilingual country means that all signposting is very carefully formulated in graphics. So public toilets, lists in buildings, even traffic signs make use of very clear symbols which will guide you on your way. For example, 'No Smoking' will be a cigarette and a pipe neatly crossed out, going up and going down will be appropriate arrows and a cafeteria might well be a small sign with a cup, a plate, a fork and a spoon. Airports and railway stations are particularly well signposted.

You will also find a person-to-person code of sign language which will quickly become clear. Swiss will tend to look you in the eyes when they address you. A sudden rolling of the eyeballs skyward means essentially that you are not understood, a flapping of the hand means try again, a nodding and shaking of the head mean here what they mean everywhere. Unlike Americans, French or Germans who will chatter on at you the blanker you look, your average Swiss is used to language problems and will pause patiently to see whether you've understood directions to a bus stop or to the infant school around the corner.

Listen carefully and slowly the language will start yielding up its codes. Repeat words that your interlocutor has emphasised even if you don't follow them. It's called learning and it's an amusing exercise that requires patience and a bit of application.

Try reading in your first weeks. The shop and road signs, obviously, will be your orientation. Pick up the local paper in the café and scan it. Look at the international news—you'll find your way round them by the landmarks of place names and the names of personalities. Look at the pictures, read the captions. Listen to the TV news.

Try reading a few months in. Comics (in the French-speaking world, these are a pretty major literary art-form, from Tintin to Tardi), magazines, and so forth. We used to buy a small stack of Maigret mysteries by Georges Siménon and patiently read them. These are great stories told in unpretentious French that will keep your reading. You'll find the equivalent in German too—browse in book stores, join the library.

Read, listen, talk, get it wrong. Enjoy it, what does it matter?

WORKING LIFE

CHAPTER 9

"One day the axe just fell."
—Bob Dylan

THE WORK ETHIC IS PRETTY IMPORTANT in Switzerland, as it is in many other European countries, and most people spend much of their time gainfully employed. It is definitely not—as it has become in parts of the US and Asia—an obsession, and people do believe very firmly in their leisure and in holidays. This does mean, of course, that if you work for an American or Asian company, for example, you'll have to be a little assertive to make sure that you get the hours and the leave to which you have the right. All companies operating in Switzerland are governed by Swiss working-condition laws, which generally limit your maximum hours (44 now, and the average person works for 41.5 hours a week) and your annual leave rights (four weeks in most jobs, five weeks if you're under 20 years of age, with the statutory holidays as well). It must be noted, on the other hand, that my sweaty-palmed compatriots have voted against adopting a universal 40-hour week on two occasions!

WAGES

Salaries often look pretty impressive on paper, but don't forget that there will be sums subtracted for various social charges (AHV/AVS national retirement fund, AI handicap allowance, in-place accident coverage and also, in many cases, withholding taxes) and that you are living in a very expensive country where money will go out as quickly as it comes in. You'd best ask about the actual take-home pay

when you are discussing salary propositions, and if you are not on withheld tax, write off about a third for this purpose.

The general pattern is that you will be given a trial period, say three months, after which your job will be stabilised. After a year or 24 months, again according to an agreement, you will be called in to the personnel office, and generally given an annual increment of salary as you gather working experience. By this time, you will have gotten to know at least some of your fellow employees, who will readily advise you on how you are being treated. The law forbids any payments below the normal Swiss salary scales applied to the job you are working in. It also entitles you to join a union, which is often a convenient way of making sure you are getting a fair deal, and to allow you the kind of representation you might need in case of difficulties and misunderstandings between you and your employers or hierarchical superiors.

Although it is true that, in theory, all qualifications being equal, women and men have the same wages, the pattern has been for women to earn less than men. The exception has generally been in the frame of state administrations, which try to set a good example. By law, a pregnancy cannot be a reason for terminating a job.

Your salary will increase if you have children, which will also entitle you to a minimum of eight weeks of maternity leave on 100 per cent pay, which can go up in some cantons if you are breastfeeding your baby. Paternity leave is beginning to be an accepted practice in some cantons, with Geneva (where the International Labour Organisation is based) taking something of a lead. Childcare from about the weaned baby stage on to preschool is available in most of the bigger centres and can be subsidised if necessary, either by your employer or by the state and municipal authorities.

HOURS OF WORK

Working hours vary considerably depending on the job. Locally, UN employees start work at 9 am, by which time many people have already been at their workplace for two hours. Lunchtime is typically pretty generous, with at least an hour being set aside. Most people finish around 5 pm or 6 pm. If you work outside of these hours on a regular basis, you are generally entitled to a shift or night-work allowance. Coffee breaks and other short absences from your workplace are generally regulated on a more or less strict basis, and there again, you will quickly and clearly be told how these things are organised. Most of the larger workplaces have a coffee corner, which these days is often non-smoking (you'll quickly find where the smokers hang out if you have that particular habit); smaller workplaces improvise or have the

Casual Interaction

I often eat with colleagues in one of the many cafés that surround my school, and looking at other tables in our cosy bistro, this seems to be the same for the bankers, panel-beaters and hairdressers of the neighbourhood.

In summer, it's even nicer—we can eat salads on a leafy terrace and listen to the inexhaustible repertoire of dirty jokes from our civil engineering professor.

occasional break in the café around the corner. This would also very often be the place of predilection to meet a client or colleague for an informal talk.

In common with practice in other parts of the world, a lot of office workers now work on a flexible-hours scheme—'glide time'—where they clock in and out in the morning and the evening, allowing for a certain time when their presence is guaranteed (generally from about 9:30 am to about 4:30 pm) to enable colleagues to contact them. In some bigger firms, employees can also arrange to do take-out and Internet-based work from their homes part of the time, an arrangement that can be useful when you have children. It can also, naturally, become very onerous as you end up with no real distinction between work and leisure—but these are your choices to make.

No, not the end of work siren, but an alphorn player—here at a feast on a Bernese alp, saying goodbye to the day.

APPEARANCE

How do you dress for work? Look around you at your workplace and fit in as best you can. Banks and law offices tend to be pretty formal—suits for gentlemen, twin sets for the ladies—but there are many offices and other administrations where a far looser dress convention applies. In outdoor and manual jobs, again, the main thing looked for is ease of movement and living. Dress also changes rather rapidly. A couple of years ago, when the school year at the polytechnic I worked for was extended into the summer months when it gets pretty hot, I was one of two members of the teaching staff who started coming to work in shorts. This caused some pretty odd comments from colleagues and one rather half-hearted—and (by me) totally ignored—attempt at a rebuke from a senior staff member which rather quickly fizzled out. Now I note that a number of colleagues turn up with some very varied legwear ranging from bermudas to South African-style business shorts with neat bobby socks. The students, mostly in shorts or light summer dresses for the girls, seem to be absorbing our wisdom with little regard to the amount of leg exposed.

GENERALLY SPEAKING

In a general way, the Swiss workplace is pretty relaxed—you pull your weight and keep your sense of humour and your normal behaviour about you and you'll be very much at ease. Almost everyone will do their best to make you comfortable, and the inevitable bitching and plotting is no worse or better than anywhere else.

What about the colour of your skin, your funny accent and all that? These things, too, must be somewhat variable, but in the workplaces I know, they hardly seem to be issues: the human resources chief is a very nice Moroccan lady who always has wonderful sweets on her table; the accountant is from the Canary Islands and seems always to be either on the way there or just back from there with a lovely tan; my delightful mathematics colleague is the son of a Mauritian nightclub dancer and was actually born in the nightclub on the night of the new year three decades ago;

the dean of communications is an energetic Vietnamese. I have a class with five African nations represented on the benches, who seem to spend much of their time slinging off at each other in English, their common language. My favourite technician is Italian of Russian origin, and I'm a Kiwi of Swiss origin whose memos in French are so odd that they cause chuckling at the direction of the institution. At least the director reads them!

So, it really isn't an issue here, at the Geneva Polytechnic Institute. Of course, it might be very different in the more hierarchical world of international agencies and business. You'll have to find out and tell me.

SWITZERLAND AT A GLANCE

CHAPTER 10

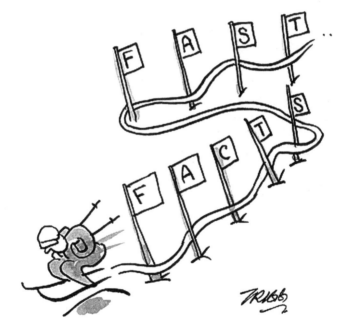

"I just said good luck."
—Bob Dylan

Official Name
Switzerland (English), Die Schweiz (German), Suisse (French), Svizzera (Italian)

Also referred to as the Swiss Confederation (English), Schweizerische Eidgenossenschaft (German), Confédération Suisse (French), Confederazione Svizzera (Italian), and Confoederatio Helvetica (Latin)

Capital
Bern (English); Bern (German); Berne (French); Berna (Italian)

Flag
A symmetrical white cross on a red background

National Anthem
Trittst im Morgenrot daher (German; original); *Sur nos monts, quand le soleil* (French); *Quando bionda aurora* (Italian)

Time
Greenwich Mean Time + 1 hour (GMT + 0100), or Central European time

Telephone Country Code
+ 41

Area
41,293 sq km (15,943 sq miles), of which some 1,500 sq km (579 sq miles) are lakes

Highest Point
Dufourspitze (4,634 m / 15,203 ft)

Land
Landlocked, Switzerland lies in central Europe with Germany to its north, France to the west, Italy to the south and south-east, and Liechtenstein and Austria to the north-east.

Climate
Central European weather with hot summers (up to 35°C), cold winters (often below 0°C, with minus 10–15°C or lower for periods in some areas), and cool, dry autumns. Good rainfall, above all in spring.

Natural Resources
Negligible mineral exploitation, some natural gas, much use of wood in all of its configurations. Vast resource of hydro-electric power using rich mountain hydrology.

Population
7,866,500 (2010 estimate)

Ethnic Groups
German (65 per cent), French (18 per cent), Italian (10 per cent), Romansch (1 per cent), others (6 per cent)

Official Languages
French, German, Italian and Romansch

Religion
Roman Catholic (41.8 per cent), Protestant (35.3 per cent), none (11.1 per cent), Muslim (4.3 per cent), unspecified (4.3 per cent), Orthodox (1.8 per cent), others (1 per cent), other Christians (0.4 per cent), based on a 2000 census.

Government
Federal republic

Administrative Divisions
26 cantons, names given below (in bold for the canton's official language or languages):

German	French	Italian
Aargau	Argovie	Argovia
Appenzell Innerrhoden	Appenzell Rhodes-Intérieures	Appenzello Interno
Appenzell Ausserrhoden	Appenzell Rhodes-Extérieures	Appenzello Esterno
Basel-Stadt	Bâle-Ville	Basilea-Città
Basel-Landschaft	Bâle-Campagne	Basilea-Campagna
Bern	**Berne**	Berna
Freiburg	**Fribourg**	Friborgo
Genf	**Genève**	Ginevra
Glarus	Glaris	Glarona
Graubünden	Grisons	**Grigioni**
Jura	**Jura**	Giura
Luzern	Lucerne	Lucerna
Neuenburg	**Neuchâtel**	Neuchâtel
Nidwalden	Nidwald	Nidvaldo
Obwalden	Obwald	Obvaldo
Schaffhausen	Schaffhouse	Sciaffusa
Schwyz	Schwyz, Schwytz	Svitto
Solothurn	Soleure	Soletta
St Gallen	Saint-Gall	San Gallo
Thurgau	Thurgovie	Turgovia
Tessin	Tessin	**Ticino**
Uri	Uri	Uri
Wallis	**Valais**	Vallese
Waadt	**Vaud**	Vaud
Zug	Zoug	Zugo
Zürich	Zurich	Zurigo

Currency
Swiss franc (CHF)

Gross Domestic Product
US$ 321.9 billion (2010 estimate)

Agricultural Products
Grains, fruits, vegetables, meat, eggs

Industries
Machinery, chemicals, watches, textiles, precision instruments, banking, tourism

Airports
In 2008, 65 in total, 42 of which have paved runways. There are three international airports: in Zürich, Geneva and Basel.

FAMOUS SWISS
The odd thing about Switzerland is that—like Belgium and Austria, for example—it has no national and linguistic identity strong enough to make its citizens recognisably Swiss to an international audience. If they were writers or thinkers, they wrote or corresponded in one of Europe's major languages; if artists, musicians or cineastes, they almost certainly did a major part of their work abroad, not asserting their Swiss origins overmuch. Add to this many famous people of foreign origin who have made their home in Switzerland and who are now considered part of Swiss culture, be they refugees or immigrants, and the situation becomes even more diffuse.

Visual Arts
So in the visual arts, for example, we would have to mention **Hans Holbein the Younger** (1497–1543) who, though born in Augsburg, made the brilliant beginnings of his career in the exciting humanist environment of Basel. His real fame, of course, came when he moved to England and was attached to the brilliant court of Henry VIII. Another Swiss who made his name in England was **Henry Fuseli** (1741–1825), who was born Johann Heinrich Füssli and a contemporary of William Blake. His *Nightmare* is a surrealistic work on a level with Goya's finest visionary paintings.

In the 20th century, an obvious candidate whom some may recognise as Swiss would be the German-born **Paul Klee** (1879–1940), who made his career initially with the Expressionists, taught for many years in the Bauhaus and was eventually forced to flee to Switzerland from Hitler in 1933. Another distinguished 'exile', **Alberto Giacometti** (1901–1966), lived many years in Paris, although he kept his roots in the Grisons region whence he came.

Artists who travelled widely but were never established for long periods—like the meticulous Genevan realist **Jean-Etienne Liotard** (1702–1789) and the Neuchâtel neoclassical and Romantic artist **Louis-Léopold Robert** (1794–1835), who studied with Jacques-Louis David in Paris—may be known to specialists but would hardly be considered household names. **Ferdinand Hodler** (1853–1918) was a fine artist whose decorations of the federal palace in Bern are a reference of high patriotic art, while the rather better known **Félix Vallotton** (1865–1925) was a more resolutely modern figure, known in our day primarily for his incomparable engraving work.

The exuberant and very popular sculptures of **Jean Tinguely** (1925–1991) rattle, jig and clatter in museums all over the world. If you like conceptual and other contemporary art, you are well served in Switzerland with suitably crazy and often elegant artists such as **Ursula Mumenthaler** (1955–) with her dislocated painted rooms, and **Pipilotti Rist** (1962–) whose sexy body art is as weird as her name. **Peter Fischli** (1952–) and **David Weiss** (1946–) do zany stuff with basement oddments, and have been shown in many international galleries.

Architects and Engineers

By far the best known Swiss architect—often mistaken for a Frenchman—is **Le Corbusier** (Charles-Édouard Jeanneret, 1887–1965), one of the great revolutionaries of the 20th century. He and the people around him attached to the CIAM (Congrès Internationaux d'Architecture Moderne), which met in a castle above Lausanne, completely changed the concept of what housing, building and cities signified.

His work—in Geneva, Marseilles and India—remains fabulous in their plasticity if not necessarily overly cosy to live in.

Another compatriot of his is the engineer **Robert Maillart** (1872–1940). You will drive over some of his spectacular realisations as you travel around Switzerland. The best known is certainly the Salginatobel Bridge, in the east of Switzerland, which was declared a World Monument by the American Society of Civil Engineers in 1991.

Francesco Borromini

Francesco Borromini (1599–1667) was born in what is now the Tessin region of Switzerland, and was a brilliant builder somewhere between an architect and an engineer, a tradition for which the Tessin-Piedmont region is still famous. His work, though—including the execution of Saint Peter's dome in Rome—was as the man with the know-how behind visionaries such as Michelangelo. It is recognised that without him, their most famous works would not have been built.

Swiss architects of our time usually make their name internationally. **Jean Tschumi** (1904–1962) and his son **Bernard Tschumi** (1944–) form something of a dynasty of great architects. The father built the magnificent lakeside headquarters of Nestlé in Vevey, and the equally sumptuous high-tech headquarters of the WHO (World Health Organisation) in Geneva. The son is best-known for the spectacular technological museum in La Vilette in Paris, and is now based in New York. **Mario Botta** (1943–), a Swiss-Italian, has a fine church in Evreux in the working class district of Paris, and a museum in San Francisco to his name, as well as many local works. **Peter Zumthor** (1943–), Botta's contemporary, has a more pronounced regional character and has done wonders using the local stone and wood of the eastern Grisons region. He has done work in Germany and the UK.

The most recent stars are **Jacques Herzog** and **Pierre de Meuron**, both born in Basel in 1950, who have together designed some of the most beautiful buildings in the last decade, including the Tate Modern in London, the Allianz Arena in Munich, and the 'Bird's Nest' stadium for the 2008 Olympics in Beijing.

An early engineer, who experimented with suspension

Inventor of Velcro

The least well-known Swiss is probably a humble electrical engineer, Georges de Mestral (1907–1990), who discovered and developed the idea of the Velcro fastener after picking seed pods out of his dog's fur on a walk in 1948. He became a discreet and highly deserving multi-millionaire.

bridges in the 19th century and who presided over the creation of first modern topographical map of Switzerland was the military man **Guillaume-Henri Dufour** (1787–1875). He is worthy of mention also because he was the general of the federal forces in Switzerland's very brief civil war of 1847 which was terminated with remarkably little bloodshed or residual bitterness. After this experience, as a friend of **Henri Dunant** (1828–1910), he was instrumental in setting up the Red Cross and the first Geneva convention for the rules of war in 1867.

Henri Dunant certainly deserves a broader mention as he is considered one of the founders of a movement for compassion and humanitarianism which was, and still is, sadly lacking in the context of wars and occasionally natural disasters. His founding experience was the aftermath of the Battle of Solferino in Italy in 1859, where he saw the horrible human waste and suffering caused by a battle, and thus set the wheels in motion for the founding of the International Red Cross. He was awarded the Nobel Peace Prize in 1901 and died, ruined and forgotten, in 1910. His movement, however, lives on, in more need of than ever in our strife-torn world.

Swiss in the Sciences

From before it even existed to now, Switzerland has a distinguished place in the world of philosophy and science. **Paracelsus** (Philipus von Hohenheim, 1493–1541) was for a long time a very distinguished teacher and scholar in Basel, and one of the inventors of modern scientific medicine.

The same city also nurtured the Bernoullis, a family of Flemish Calvinist origins who produced two generations of mathematicians and physicists whose names are used far more often in theoretical and applied science, fluid dynamics and aviation than as the men of science they were.

Skiers have two options to get to the top of the peak: enclosed ski lifts such as this, or open chair lifts.

Small charming buildings that date back a few centuries can be found in each of the 26 cantons in Switzerland. This street in Bern makes an attractive picture, decorated with flags representing the different cantons.

The country is known to be a banking haven and its many banks provide a variety of discreet services to their clientele which comprises the world's rich and famous.

CREDI

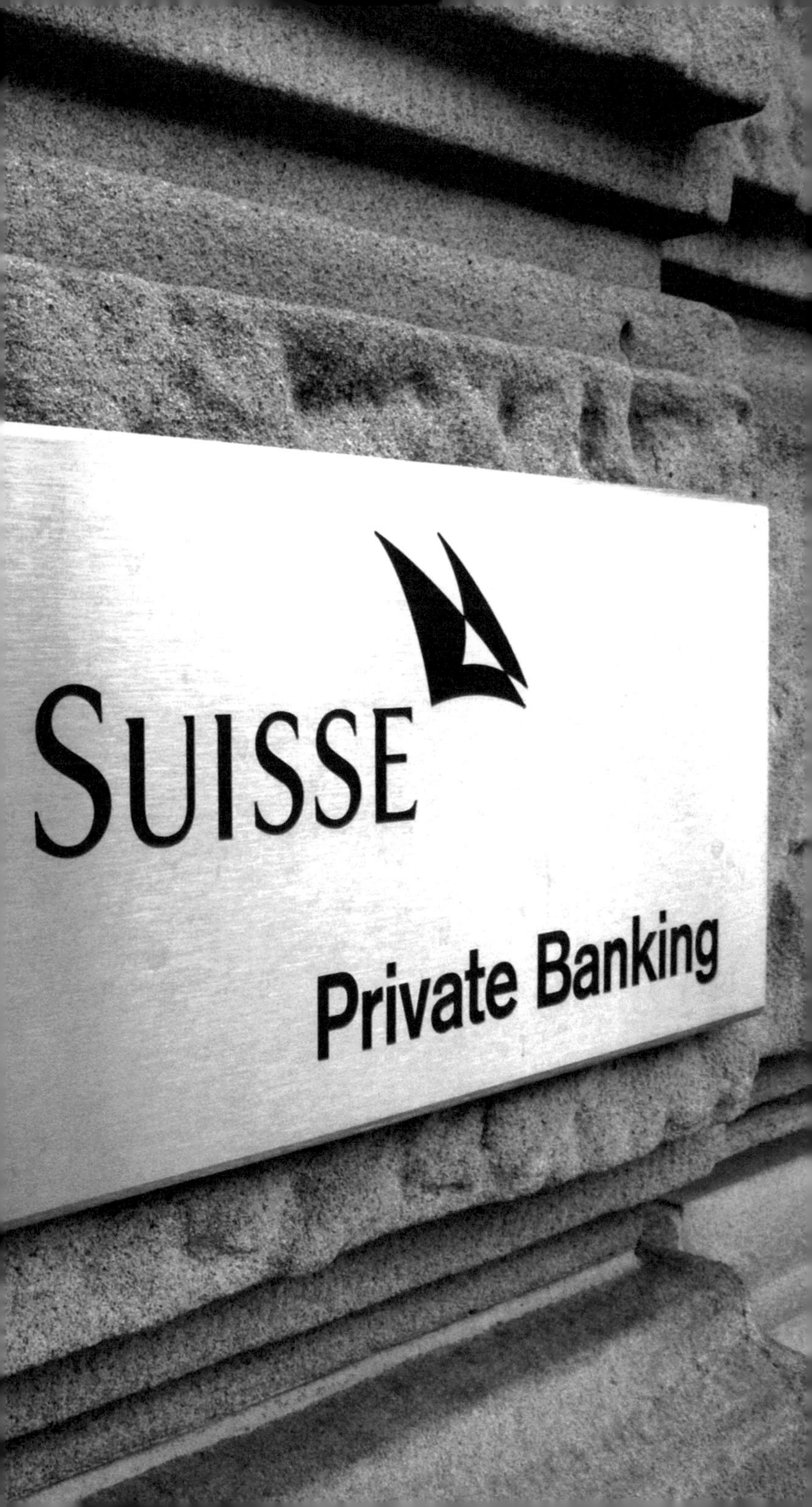
SUISSE
Private Banking

Often associated with Switzerland, the alphorn has its origins in medieval times, when it was used across the mountainous regions of Europe for communication.

Zurich Airport in Kloten is the country's largest international air gateway. A railway station located underneath the terminal building provides train connections to most parts of Switzerland.

Jakob Bernoulli (1654–1705) and his brilliant kid brother **Johann Bernoulli** (1667–1748) seem to have made a very important contribution to the field of algebra. **Leonhard Euler** (1707–1783), a student of Jakob Bernoulli in Basel, became another world-renowned mathematician and philosopher. He was eventually a professor of physics and maths at Saint Petersburg Academy, as part of a very exciting Russian renaissance in the late 18th century. **Hans Bernoulli** (1876–1959) is another of the family who, as an architect, built one of Switzerland's first garden cities in Riehen near the family's Basel home.

Albert Einstein

A genius of the stature of Albert Einstein (1879–1955) probably transcends mere categories such as nationality. Yet be it known that he was granted Swiss citizenship in 1901, a German passport in 1914 and finally died an American. Moreover, the bulk of his most exciting work on relativity was done when he was working for the Swiss patent office in Bern, a humble tentacle in the polyp of Swiss federal bureaucracy.

In a similar vein, we could mention the de Saussure family in Geneva. **Horace Bénedict de Saussure** (1740–1799) was essentially a physicist and geologist. He was professor at the Academy of Geneva from 1762–1786, and is famous for his studies of the geology, meteorology and botany of the mountainous regions of Europe, particularly the nearby French Alps. He is the first person to have climbed Europe's highest summit, Mont Blanc. His mountain exploits and pioneering scientific observations are described in his great work, *Voyages dans les Alpes* (4 volumes, 1779). A generation on, **Ferdinand de Saussure** (1857–1913)—grandson of Horace and son of the distinguished biochemist **Nicolas-Théodore de Saussure** (1767–1845)—was to be the founder of modern structural linguistics, which attempted to describe the structure of language rather than the history of particular languages and language forms.

Many, many distinguished Germans set up house in Switzerland, often to get away from the storms of strife and war there. So the great writer **Hermann Hesse** (1877–1962)—his first wife was Maria Bernoulli, sister of Hans Bernoulli of Basel—lived the largest part of his turbulent life here, and was naturalised in 1926. Fellow Nobel-winner **Thomas Mann**

(1875–1955) stayed a decade before the war and eventually returned from California during the McCarthy witch-hunt and died near Zürich in 1955.

Hesse's first wife brings us to another famous Swiss, **Carl Gustav Jung** (1875–1961), who treated her for schizophrenia. Jung's contribution to the understanding of the psyche by symbols and archetypes is a fascinating study, and adds another facet to the research on the mind pioneered by his teacher and subsequent rival Sigmund Freud.

Literary Figures

Before the 20th century, Swiss writers who were known out of the country are not many. So, although **Jean-Jacques Rousseau** (1712–1778)—the great prophetic writer on economics and liberty—was born into a Genevan watchmaker's family, this would not have identified him as Swiss, for Geneva was then an independent city state, linked to the Swiss only by ad-hoc trade and defence pacts. It seems, though, that in the salons of Paris he was known for his Genevan accent.

From the last generation, two writers who'd be known outside of Switzerland are the great dramatists **Friedrich Dürrenmatt** (1921–1990) and **Max Frisch** (1911–1991), in the latter case, also as a novelist—his 1954 *Stiller* remains a classic. Writers for the stage, their works have spread by translations and productions throughout the world. Dürrenmatt's best known piece is *The Visit*, a corrosive play of 1956. Frisch's major play is probably *The Fire Raisers* (1953), a marvellous parable on political indifference.

Albert Cohen (1895–1981) was a Greek-born Jewish novelist who wrote in French, as befitted a Genevan. His *Belle du Seigneur* (1968) is set in the world of the League of Nations in that city. Later authors whose work is known beyond Switzerland's borders would be the Paris-based investigative journalist **Niklaus Meienberg** (1940–1993), part of the post-1968 wave of protest against the complacency and hypocrisy of the peaceful and unruffled little republic. The Zurichois **Paul Nizon** (1929–) has also been exiled in Paris for three decades, writing solidly, while the French-Swiss writer **Jacques Chessex** (1934–) seems to have remained better known locally.

The Great Musicians

In music, Switzerland's contribution is again pretty modest, commensurate with its size. **Jean-Jacques Rousseau** dabbled in music, and the Genevan **Émile Jaques-Dalcroze** (1865–1950) was very influential in introducing music and rhythm into the school curriculum, and it is to him we owe the concept of 'eurhythmics'—using rhythmic body movements to understand music. The best known serious composer, **Arthur Honegger** (1892–1955), was born in France of Zürichois parents and worked mainly in the French modernist context. His fine oratorio *King David* (1921) first opened in Morat, Switzerland and is now very much part of the international repertoire.

The most famous Swiss musician is surely conductor **Ernest Ansermet** (1883–1969), who premiered many of Igor Stravinsky's symphonic works and who created Switzerland's finest orchestra, the Geneva-based Orchestre de la Suisse Romande. We should also mention **Alfred-Denis Cortod** (1877–1962), one of the greatest pianists and piano teachers of all time, and many singers such as the soprano **Lisa della Casa** (1919–), a superlative interpreter of Strauss and Mozart, who was born in Burgdorf, Bern, and the operatic tenor **Ernst Haefliger** (1919–2007).

Pop music, in its various manifestations, is very much alive here. One of the better known singers, **Stephan Eicher** (1960–), who's been active for a couple of decades, happily warbles in three languages: English, French and Swiss-German.

Stage and Screen

What about actors? The grandfather of them all is that magnificent dirty old man **Michel Simon** (1895–1975), born in Geneva. He was associated with many of Jean Renoir's films and Jean Vigo's *Atlante* (1934) and appeared in countless films almost to his death. Then, for the older gentlemen, there is the curvaceous **Ursula Andress**

Business and Finance

I know very little about banking and business, but I'm sure there must be Swiss names which have transcended the borders, as Swiss money and Swiss stock certainly do. Two names that seem to come up are Daniel Borel (1950–) of Logitech, the mouse man who has certainly made a big impact with a worldwide business, and Ernesto Bertarelli (1965–), the Swiss-Italian director of the big Genevan-based biotech firm Sereno, who is known internationally for having pinched the America's Cup in international sailing from favourites New Zealand in 2003.

(1936–), above all known for her participation in two James Bond classics—*Dr No* and *Casino Royale*—in the mid-60s. In the same generation, and still very much active, is the versatile and brilliant **Bruno Ganz** (1941–), now mainly living in Germany and working as a stage actor as well. He has been in films by Eric Rohmer, Werner Herzog, **Alain Tanner** (another Swiss, 1929–) and of course, Wim Wenders. In the younger generation, **Vincent Perez** (1962–), of Swiss-Spanish extraction, is worth a look. His work with **Isabelle Adjani** (a Swiss resident of Algerian origin, 1955–) under French director Patrice Chéreau in the very violent *La Reine Margot* (1994) is incomparable.

Probably the only Swiss film director known outside of Switzerland is the brilliant if exasperating **Jean-Luc Godard** (1930–), who was born to a Swiss-French family in Paris but has been a Swiss citizen and resident for most of his life. His films are a legendary component of the French 'New Wave' of the 1950s and early 1960s. Essentially, they used the filmic medium as a means of agitation in the existentialist mode, from *Breathless* (1960) to *In Praise of Love* (2001).

In theatre directing, the names of **Benno Besson** (1922–2006), born in Yverdon, and **Matthias Langhoff** (1941–), in Zürich of German refugee parents, are internationally known. Both have done brilliant things locally and at the Berliner Schaubühne—Brecht's mythical theatre—as well as in other world centres.

Other Artistic Areas

Some Swiss are known for unusual reasons. Two clowns, **Grock** (1880–1959) and, a generation later, the genial Swiss-Italian **Dimitri** (1935–), have had us laughing at their antics, and moved by their wonderful humanity. **Emil Steinberger** (1933–) is a hilarious one-man act, known out of Switzerland mainly by his first name and for a few acting roles in films.

Emil Bührle (1890–1956), heir of the Bührle armaments fortune, is known chiefly for his fabulous art collection currently housed in a villa museum in Zürich. Those who know how he got his money might be a little less than happy about visiting the collection, but most major art collections, and even museums aren't exactly squeaky clean when we look into their history.

A Swiss name familiar to specialists in the book and printing world would be **Adrian Frutiger** (1928–), one of the most inventive and imaginative typeface designers known. 'Univers' is but one of his countless contributions, and his teaching on the clarity and metalanguage of typefaces remains indispensable.

In my own domain, photography, the best-known Swiss is probably the Zurichois **Robert Frank** (1924–). His book, *The Americans* (1958)—a landmark in photographic art—chronicles in a series of grainy documentary images his travels across the United States with Beat poet Jack Kerouac, who also wrote the text for the book. Another travelling photographer associated with Magnum Photos (a photographers' co-operative) is **Werner Bischoff** (1916–1954), whose images from South America and Asia remain legendary; and the bluff, humorous **René Burri** (1933–) is still active with the agency. **Michael von Graffenried** (1957–) is a fine contemporary photographer with a very clear humanistic message; his latest work focuses on Algeria. **Christian Vogt** (1944–) is a Basel-based photographer, probably the finest in my generation. Of course much of modern photography has found its way into mainstream contemporary art as elsewhere in the world.

Sports
Switzerland is a small country, which makes it a little difficult to pool resources for really great international sporting achievements. In skiing, surprisingly, the Swiss

have been very much in the 'also ran' category in the last few decades, well behind their Austrian, French, Italian and US peers. There has been one important name in Swiss motor racing, the Fribourgeois **Jo (Joseph) Siffert** (1936–1971), who crashed to his death in the UK, much to the grief of his school friend, the sculptor Jean Tinguely.

The individual sport in which Swiss have excelled is tennis, with the Czech-born star **Martina Hingis** (1980–), a crafty, imaginative player, dominating women's tennis in the 1990s until the US rolled out the Williams sisters. The Balois **Roger Federer** (1981–) seems to have no such worries. For four years running (2004–2007), he finished at the top of the world rankings, and now holds a men's record of 16 Grand Slam singles titles. His playing is diabolically efficient but never nasty.

For team sports, football (soccer) is very popular here, but again, the Swiss national side is not exactly overwhelming on the field. Individual clubs are attached to most urban centres (such as Grasshoppers in Zürich and Xamax in Neuchâtel) and there is a national league played every year with a good following.

Resident Swiss

Another chapter could be written on famous people who have lived or are still residing here. Two centuries ago, you might have come across **Lord Byron** (1788–1824) and the Shelleys horsing around in their spacious Geneva home, where **Mary Shelley** (1797–1851) created her gothic novel, *Frankenstein* (1818). A little later **George Eliot** (1819–1880), **Mikhail Aleksandrovich Bakunin** (1814–1876) and **Joseph Conrad** (1857–1924) all made their homes here at one time or another. **Henry James** (1843–1916) walked around the lake, **Sir Leslie Stephen** (Virginia Woolf's father, the lexicographer, 1832–1904), and **John Ruskin** (1819–1900) clambered about

Visiting Royalty

Many of the families of rich oil sheikhs and even Arab royalty have settled here, occasionally buying a castle here, a hotel there or the controlling shares of a business. The big annual firework feast in Geneva fills the five-star hotels with very large extended families who watch the marvellous event spellbound.

the mountains. The last was at loggerheads with **Eugène-Emmanuel Viollet-le-Duc** (1814–1879), the French architect who restored Lausanne's cathedral into one of the glories of the Gothic Revival.

The realist painter **Camille Corot** (1796–1875) often stayed with friends in Switzerland. **Benito Mussolini** (1883–1945) was thrown out of Lausanne for agitating and misbehaving as a young man. **F. Scott Fitzgerald** (1896–1940), too, spent some time here. That great exile **James Joyce** (1882–1941), one of many World War II refugees, died in Zürich in 1941. A number of French intellectuals came here after World War II to escape the rather loathsome stuff they'd written during the war, notably **Paul Morand** (1888–1976). **Georges Siménon** (1903–1989), the Belgian creator of the detective Maigret, lived in Switzerland most of his life for tax reasons, and the great Russian-American writer **Vladimir Nabokov** (1899–1977) enjoyed the comfort of a lakeside luxury hotel in Montreux for the last three decades of his life. **Charlie Chaplin** (1889–1977)—whose daughter Geraldine was born in Switzerland and currently makes her home here—had a house of his own down the road from Nabokov.

Sadruddin Aga Khan (1933–) has a salubrious property on Lake Geneva, and **Audrey Hepburn** (1929–1993) lived for many years in Byron's old villa. **David Niven** (1909–1983) and **Elizabeth Taylor** (1932–2011) both lived near Gstaad and had, so we are told, many epic parties there. The latter's celebrated ex-husband, **Richard Burton** (1925–1984) lived his later years in a picturesque village on the lake.

In the old town of Geneva, **Andrés Segovia** (1893–1987), the guitarist, had an apartment with a terrace within hearing distance of the Argentinian writer and philosopher, **Jorge Luis Borges** (1899–1986), who is buried here. The French cellist **Pierre Fournier** (1906–1986) also lived in Geneva not far from the lake. Once or twice, we saw the legendary jazz diva **Nina Simone** (1933–2003). She lived her rather sad last years exiled from the United States, whose racism and politics she found repugnant.

The French-Canadian singer **Céline Dion** (1968–) lives quietly in Zürich between star concerts; film actors **Isabelle**

Adjani and **Alain Délon** (1935–) in Geneva, as well as **Phil Collins** (1951–) of the wonderful voice and drumbeat, whose kids attend the village school where he lives.

David Bowie (1947–) chills out in Lausanne between his spectacular star engagements. Formula One racing drivers **Alain Prost** (1955–) and **Michael Schumacher** (1969–) have settled in different regions of Switzerland. All this is good news for the Swiss taxman, who does not ignore these good folks—although he does not trouble them too much either. It is also good news for Switzerland, because many of these people discreetly ginger up local cultural life.

ACRONYMS IN SWITZERLAND

Thousands of acronyms are in daily use, and the situation is complicated by their being in three or four languages. Here is a selection of the most commonly encountered:

AHV/AVS/AI	Alter und Hinterlassenenversicherung (German), Assurance pour la Vieillesse et Assurance Invalidité (French). The federal retirement and handicap compensation fund.
CFF	Chemin de Fer Fédéral. Switzerland's legendary federal railway network.
CH	Confoederatio Helvetica (Latin). An international code to denote the Swiss confederation, used on automobile plates, Internet domain names, and other official contexts.
CERN	Centre Européen pour la Récherche Nucléaire. The European Nuclear Research Centre, located in Geneva.
CNA	Caisse Nationale d'Assurance (French). A national accident insurance scheme.
HB	The international civil aircraft country code for Switzerland (and Liechtenstein).
IATA	International Air Transport Association
PKW	Personenkraftwagen. A rather odd German vestige which simply means a saloon car.
RC	Résponsabilité civile (French), or Privathaftpflicht (German). Third-party damage insurance that is

	compulsory for car and dog registration; highly recommended for household insurance.
RSI	Radiotelevisione svizzera di lingua italiana, the Italian-language broadcaster.
SBB	Schweizer Bundesbahn, the Swiss federal railway network.
SPS/PSS	Sozialdemokratische Partei der Schweiz (German), Parti Socialiste Suisse (French), Partito Socialista Svizzero (Italian), Social Democratic Party of Switzerland (English).
SUVA	Schweizerische Unfallversichwerung (German). A national accident insurance scheme.
SF 1 & 2	Schweizer Fernsehen, the two German-language public TV channels.
TSR 1 & 2	Télévision Suisse Romande, the two French-language public TV channels.
UBS	Union Bank of Switzerland (English); Schweizerische Bankgesellschaft (German), Union de Banques Suisses (French), Unione di Banche Svizzere (Italian). It merged with the Swiss Banking Corporation in 1998 and is now known as UBS AG.
UDC	The Swiss People's Party, or Democratic Union of the Centre, Schweizerische Volkspartei (German), Union Démocratique du Centre (French), Unione Democratica di Centro (Italian).
VO	Version originale. A term used to describe films shown at the cinema in their original languages.

PLACES OF INTEREST
Aarau
Rather bland, except for a splendid museum of Swiss art from the 18th century. Close to the Hapsburg ruins, and surrounded by lovely rolling hills with beech forests.

Appenzell
A small place peopled by folk who do amazing things with whittled wood.

Bern

The capital of Switzerland, Bern is a city at ease in both the French and German languages. It's a comfortable, delightful old town with many little cafés where coffee is served in stem glasses. Here, you will find a clock tower from the 14th century—the Zytgloggeturm—as well as the wondrous new Paul Klee Museum designed by Renzo Piano.

La Chaux des Fonds

Amazing landscapes on the Jura plateau.

Chur

Switzerland's oldest city, and capital of the canton of Graubünden/Grisons—which, with its remote valleys, is one of the most stunning places imaginable.

Basel

Basel is a big and very international place, located on the border of three countries. It's a pleasant, congenial city, not unlike Strasbourg, with a wonderful cathedral and good food, with Swiss-German and Alsatian-French influences. Basel has many museums and a strong cultural background. A university with a world-famous medical school is located here.

Brig

Town perched on two peaks. Best seen from afar.

Delémont

Capital of the Jura canton—Switzerland's youngest canton, carved after much struggling out of Bern. Delémont is very French-speaking and is a gateway to some of the most beautiful regions between Switzerland and France.

Frauenfeld

A rather boring town in the east that is famous for its excellent stainless steel kitchenware called Sigg and horse races. It is also the author's birthplace, and I'm waiting for the equestrian statue to be commissioned.

Fribourg
A hilltop city within cannon range of Bern that is home to Switzerland's most important Catholic university and a lovely Catholic cathedral.

Geneva
A fine, if slightly self-important city, beautifully set on the lake of the same name. Very important internationally with the Red Cross and the United Nations, as well as a number of other international organisations. Ironically, it is the least Swiss place in Switzerland. Also home to great opera and music venues and hosts the Orchestre de la Suisse Romande made famous by Ernest Ansermet.

Gruyère
Spectacular hilltop town famous for its cheese, with a castle overlooking a lake. On Sundays, the men have been known to wear black waistcoats and quaint little caps, and occasionally burst into song.

Lausanne
Impressive hill city on Lake Léman that has a fine restored Gothic cathedral, an important university and polytechnic college, a great photo museum, as well as the Museum of Art Brut. A superb chamber orchestra plays here.

Luzern
A friendly, good-humoured city located between two lakes that boasts a famous wooden bridge, Baroque cathedral and the best concert hall in the country.

Martigny
The gateway to the French and Italian Alps, and home to the Gianadda art museum.

Montreux
Located on Lake Geneva, Montreux is a wonderful Riviera-like place that hosts an annual jazz festival.

Neuchâtel
Great little city on its very own lake that can boast of having the best ethnographic museum in Switzerland.

Olten
The place where the railway lines cross, and home to beautiful ladies, according to some people.

St Gallen
A city with staggering scenery, this is the site of one of the finest libraries and Baroque churches in the world. Its university is Switzerland's most important centre of economic and business studies.

Solothurn
A charming lakeside place with some preposterous medieval fortifications but a fine watchmaking tradition.

Schwytz
Capital of the canton of the same name. Beautiful setting and the gateway to Zürich from the central Alps.

Winterthur
Surprising town tucked in behind Zürich. Discreet and pleasant, its old industrial buildings are important cultural centres now. Museums of fine arts and photography are also to be found here.

Zürich
The big one. You name it, Zürich's got it, usually in several examples. Well-located on a lake and a river, Zürich has a good university and polytechnic and is important for international trade fairs. Worth a visit.

Zug
City or canton, take your pick. Pretty if boring place known for its low income taxes and its delicious cherry brandy, kirsch. It is also known for a legendary chocolate cake—which you may be able to afford after you get your tax rebates.

CULTURE QUIZ

SITUATION 1
You had an important presentation to give outside your workplace, and the person who invited you made a complete dog's breakfast of the arrangements. The Powerpoint presentation took a quarter of an hour to get going while important people sat fidgeting around the table—in a dingy basement room he managed to scrape up for you. You finally give a brilliant presentation, of course. But what do you do afterwards?

Ⓐ You get the management of your outfit to write a polite but firm letter to the management of the host firm, pointing out that a more serious approach would be appreciated to avoid misunderstandings in the future.

Ⓑ You quietly but efficiently tear a strip of the person responsible after the presentation.

Ⓒ You send him an email the next day, thanking him but pointing out that things could have been better prepared.

Ⓓ You ignore the whole business; the bottom line is that the host firm would probably have realised that they had made a gaffe, and your presentation went across in the end.

Comments
A lot will depend on the relations you have with the institution. **Ⓐ** seems rather excessive and might taint further business relations between you and the other outfit. Letters in European practice are pretty high level and seem to count as virtually legal documents if they bear a date and a signature. **Ⓑ** seems like a waste of time. The guy must know he's messed up. **Ⓒ** would be the most diplomatic (without copies up the hierarchy), or possibly leave it at **Ⓓ**, in the hope of receiving some kind of acknowledgement and apology from the responsible chap later.

SITUATION 2

You can't sleep; the people in the apartment above yours are obviously having a pretty major squabble at two in the morning. And it's not the first time.

Ⓐ Right, let's settle this now. You put on a dressing gown and shuffle upstairs, knock on their door and put on your sweetest sleepy face when they open, muttering something about needing to sleep.

Ⓑ You telephone the local police post and get transferred to a busy switchboard and are asked if you want to make a complaint.

Ⓒ You speak to the concierge (*Hauswart*) the next day and ask him or her what can be done.

Ⓓ You curl up and try to get back to sleep.

Comments

Almost impossible to come up with an answer that is 'right', so much depends on the circumstances. What are you built like—a hulking rugby forward or a delicate little secretary? What are the neighbours like—utter brutes or just a little overexcited? Have you met the janitor before? Is there a real and immediate danger of violence or injury? We have had recourse to **Ⓐ**, **Ⓒ** and **Ⓓ** with varying success. You'd only use **Ⓑ** if stuff or people start flying out of the windows. Certainly if the slinging matches become too much of a habit, you'll have to speak to the concierge or the housing agent. There is always the hope, of course, that if they scream at each other so much, they won't stay together for very long; but don't be too sure of that either.

SITUATION 3

Young Eric is in Standard 3 at the local primary school and seems to be getting more and more stressed out by the workload his teacher gives him—endless screeds of homework that keep him hunched over his table in the evenings when other kids are out playing.

A You drop in and see the teacher and try to reason with her.

B You talk to the head of the school and try to see whether this is the norm.

C You talk to other parents in Eric's class and see what their experience is. You find out if there is a parent-teacher association.

D You write a letter to the teacher concerned, giving your point of view clearly and firmly.

Comments

C would be best. As a stranger in the local school system (as will be up to 30–40 per cent of the parents in a city school, by the way), the best thing to do is to chat with other parents of kids in his class and see whether their reaction is the same. They might also have children in other classes and will be more able to make comparisons. There probably is a PTA which might be quite effective, but try to involve them only if you have already been in touch with them. Listening to other parents, you will get a clearer vision of what to do next. It would be helpful to speak with the teacher in a more general way, and delicately bring up the subject eventually. Only if she proves recalcitrant should you contemplate options **B** or **D**.

SITUATION 4

Oops, it had to happen sooner or later. The man with the wee badge catches you on the tram without a valid ticket. You had a ticket, but it has run out. The fine will be 50 Swiss francs, thank you. So you:

A Look at him under your lovely fluttering eyelashes, adjust your miniskirt and lisp something incomprehensible at him in your foreign tongue.

B Shut up and pay up.

C Take him to task, explain that your ticket has only just run out and you were getting off at the next stop anyway (a hideous lie that) and anyway you've got your rights, etc.

D Pull the emergency door switch, jump, and run as fast as your fleet Nikes can carry you. He's middle-aged and overweight, so you're away!

Comments

❸ obviously. You can try the others but you'll be busted sooner or later for ❹; the cities are so small here that the fellow will probably catch up with you in time. You'll lose out and probably have to pay extra on ❸ and you've seriously dented your chances of eternal heavenly bliss as well. ❹ might work, but I have serious doubts.

SITUATION 5

This is based on an actual situation. It's a lovely sunny day in the park. You're sitting on the grass, on your own, with a book on economic history. Thirty or forty other people are decorously scattered around. You think of your family back in Cameroon. Suddenly, a guy in plainclothes comes up and tells you that you aren't allowed to sit on the grass, didn't you see the sign, please move on. You realise that this is an officer of the municipal park board.

❹ You close your book, get up, and quietly and sadly move away.

❸ You smile vacantly and ask him for an identity card, note his name and then saunter off. Later, you write a letter to the municipal authorities, copy to SOS Racisme.

❸ You don't move or react and see what happens.

❹ You understandably get angry and tell him that you are one of dozens of people here and that his act is racist.

Comments

Of course, there's no doubt about it, this is blatant racism, which unfortunately grows like a nasty weed in the cracks of this smooth country. The person who told me this opted for option ❸ and eventually got an apology from the city authorities, who told him that they'd reprimanded the park attendant. The following summer, incidentally, the green space in parks was opened up for people to use, provided they did not mess it up. He tells me he was tempted to try option ❸, a kind of passive resistance option. The man would hardly have assaulted him, and could not have fetched the police without getting himself into deep trouble. Switzerland

has very clear and strictly applied anti-racism laws. Option
D would probably have worked for him as well, as most of
the other park users would have shared his outrage, but he
says 'They all looked so peaceful and happy'. He's obviously
too decent.

SITUATION 6

One of the hotplates on your kitchen stove, which came with
the apartment, seems to have given up the ghost. You'll have
to get the ceramic plate changed and reinstalled.

A You saw that the electrical goods shop down the road had
  similar stove tops for sale at a good price. You go down
  and buy one with the installation price included, and send
  the bill to the housing agent.
B You ring the housing agent and ask for a repairman to
  be sent out. It means cooking on three plates for a good
  week.
C You ask the janitor what to do, and follow his advice to get
  in touch with the electrical firm that handles these things
  for the building.
D You cook on three plates until your lease runs out.

Comments

Whatever you do, don't even try option **D**: the housing agent
will bust you for the cost of a replacement stove top when
you leave, and charge it on your escrowed rent deposit. **A**
is not a good idea either; it might be a little cheaper and
faster than the other options, but the housing agent will not
be obligated to cover an expense that he or she has not
agreed on, and which was incurred by someone who did
not have a maintenance contract for the building. Which
leaves **C** and **B**, in that order.

DO'S AND DON'TS

DO'S

- Do accept Switzerland as it is. It's been around for maybe 700 years, and is a comfortable and pleasant enough place in which to live.

- Do try to fit in at a local level. Listen to people, engage with local issues once you understand them, and you will soon make friends and have a lot of exciting stuff going.

- Do what you can to find local outlets for your interests, hobbies or sport. There is no better way to get to know people in a place than doing things with them.

- Do tactfully but clearly let it be known where you come from. This is ultimately far better than becoming a target for gossip from the more bigoted members of the population.

- Do keep up a sense of humour and detachment as regards everyday life and its hassles.

- Do respect laws and institutions. Even if you transgress them, as we all do, you must at least have a sense of where the line is drawn

- Do fit in with the Swiss work ethic of being on time and doing as best you can the tasks that you are set or that impose themselves.

- Do engage in and respect the particularities of mores and practices in the canton in which you settle.

- Do go to bed at 10 pm—a slightly exaggerated take on Switzerland's obsession with having quiet nights.

- Do trim your hedges, cut your lawn, put the garbage out in regulation bags and generally tidy up where you live—in conformity with what the neighbourhood does, or the by-laws. As a 'foreigner', you will have some people keeping a less than benevolent eye on you.

- Do make an effort to be a good and reasonable neighbour in your block of flats. A little issue like not returning the keys of the collective laundry room can blow up into quite an unedifying situation.

- Do make an effort to learn a minimum of the language and culture of your adopted canton.
- Do live your life with dignity. Have your fun but assert yourself if you feel you are being unjustly or oddly treated.
- Do make sure you are doing your best to abide by any regulations that the immigration authorities impose on you. A delay must be respected, a letter must be answered, a convocation must be kept.

DON'TS

- Don't try to change Switzerland into a country you would like it to be.
- Don't put your nose or your voice into national affairs until you have been here some years. The whole political system is based on small entities, and national policy is something of an exclusion zone unless you have lived here and established yourself well.
- Don't avoid all local contact. You will only arouse suspicion and gossip.
- Don't hang out exclusively with people of your own nationality. You may be more comfortable with them, but it is more fun, and ultimately healthier, to widen your network of friends.
- Don't get uptight about matters you can do nothing about.
- Don't provoke others unnecessarily. Here, as elsewhere, people like a quiet life and have put in place structures that run reasonably smoothly.
- Don't make a religion of work. You will be respected if you stand up for your right to leisure time and a reasonable level of work or studies.
- Don't expect homogeneity. Even admitting that Switzerland is a small country, it is very diverse in its languages, secular and religious patterns and general attitude to life.
- Don't provoke the ire of fellow tenants by trivial actions such as not putting your garbage out, leaving a mess by your door and so on. There are always very clear rules posted—worth a look at to live in peace with everyone in your building.

- Don't expect to be understood in the language of your origin, especially in the countryside.
- Don't make a show of you 'foreignness' by, say, draping a flag off your balcony. There are occasions when you are justified in doing so, like at a football match, but otherwise you are best off keeping a 'normal' profile in dress and behaviour. Much of this book deals with these issues and what constitutes 'normal'.

GLOSSARY

I find that the use of phrasebook phrases is counterproductive: in most cases, the Swiss will have some knowledge of English, and attempts to speak one of the national languages will either provoke puzzlement or an incomprehensible reply, which will have you looking for advice elsewhere.

Dialects are another ballgame, especially with Swiss-Germans, where there are very important variants in the words. And in more popular circles, a city-slicker word used in a country context might produce some rather less than positive reactions. With these provisos here goes.

For Swiss-German, I give both the written form—which is congruous with Standard German—and the pronunciation as you will hear it in Switzerland (in brackets).

NUMBERS

	German	French	Italian
1	eins (eis)	un	uno
2	zwei	deux	due
3	drei (drü)	trois	tre
4	vier	quatre	quattro
5	fünf (füüf)	cinq	cinque
6	sechs (sächs)	six	sei
7	sieben (sibe)	sept	sette
8	acht	huit	otto
9	neun (nün)	neuf	nove
10	zehn (zäh)	dix	dieci
11	elf	onze	undici
12	zwölf	douze	dodici
13	dreizehn (drizäh)	treize	tredici
17	siebzehn (sibzäh)	dix-sept	diciassette
20	zwanzig (zwänzg)	vingt	venti
30	dreissig (drissg)	trente	trenta
100	hundert	cent	cento

COMMON PHRASES

English	German
Hello.	*Grüezi.*
Good morning.	*Guete Morge. Guete Tag.*
Good evening.	*Guete Abig.*
Good night (bedtime).	*Guet Nacht.*
Thank you.	*Merci vielmal. Danke.*
No, thank you.	*Nei, danke. Nei, merci.*
Where is...	*Wo ist... (Wo isch...)*
...the toilet?	*...s'WC?*
...the exit?	*...der Ausgang (Usgang)?*
...the station?	*...der Bahnhof?*
There's been an accident.	*S'isch an Unglück passiert.*
We need an ambulance.	*Wir brauchen einen Krankenwagen.*
We need the police.	*Wir brauchen die Polizei.*

DIRECTIONS

English	German
right	*rechts*
left	*links*
straight ahead	*graadus*
up	*ufe, obe*
down	*abe, dunne*
around	*rundu*
in, inside	*im / dinne*

French	Italian
Bonjour. Salut.	*Buon giorno. Salve.*
Bonjour.	*Buon giorno.*
Bonsoir.	*Buona sera.*
Bonne nuit.	*Buona notte.*
Merci.	*Grazie.*
Non, merci.	*No, grazie.*
Où se trouve... / Où est...	*Dov'è...*
...les toilettes?	*...la gabinetta?*
...la sortie?	*...l'uscita?*
...la gare?	*...la stazione?*
Un accident s'est passé.	*C'è stato un incidente.*
Il faut une ambulance.	*Abbiamo bisogno di un'ambulanza.*
Il faut appeler la police.	*Dov'è la policia?*

French	Italian
droite	*destra*
gauche	*sinistra*
tout droit	*dritto / sempre dritto*
en haut / vers le haut	*su*
en bas / vers le bas	*giù / laggiù*
autour	*intorno / in giro per*
dans / dedans	*in*

RESOURCE GUIDE

EMERGENCY NUMBERS

Police	117
Fire Service	118
Ambulance	144
International Emergency	112
Vehicle Rescue	140
REGA Air Rescue	1414
Toxic poisoning	145
Samaritans	143

USEFUL ADDRESSES

Immigration and practical information about visas, stays etc.

- Comparis is a brilliant site, carefully researched and updated to the minute, loaded with practical information about all aspects of life in Switzerland. http://en.comparis.ch/comparis
- http://travel-island.com/immigrationvisa/switzerland.html

These two international lawyers specialise in immigration and business implantation in the country.

- Micheloud & Cie Grand-Chêne
  8 CH-1003 Lausanne
  Tel: + 41 21 331 48 48
- Sgier und Partner GmbH
  Gartenstrasse 36, 8002 Zürich
  Tel: + 41 (0)44 228 78 90
  E-mail: info@sgierpartner.ch

Language Courses

The best known courses—and good value-for-money—are probably the one attached to the Migros supermarket chains and some of the big Berlitz related centres.

- http://www.klubschule.ch
  This Migros site, giving addresses of schools in 50 centres, is rather coyly named.

- http://www.languageschoolsguide.com
- http://www.inlingua.ch is a Swiss school using the Berlitz method.

Accommodation and Job-hunting
Tenants & legal protection, other services.

- http://www.asloca.ch
  http://www.mieterverband.ch
  The most efficient tenants protection association. It is organised on a cantonal basis with a centre for each linguistic region as well.
- http://www.swisslawyers.com/ge
  With a branch in every canton, a similar arrangement to Asloca, you are able to get initial legal advice at a reduced price for any legal problem that may confront you.

Practical Questions

- http://www.cagi.ch/en
  A useful little site based in Geneva and directed above all at the very large international community active in various UN and other bureaux here. Available in English and French. Good down-to-earth advice on everything, many links.
- http://www.admin.ch/ch
  The mother of all sites, an official central government site which gives you tons of information though little advice. It will also put you onto the sites of the 25 cantons which are invariably very rich in the more practical questions concerning your life there.
- http://www.swisspolitics.org
  Useful way of keeping abreast of what is going on at any time, new legislation, *votations* and other changes.
- http://www.englishforum.ch
  English Forum seems to have been of use to some of our English-speaking friends. Occasionally descends into bitching sessions, but nevertheless comes up with a lot of good advice on practical matters that is usually right.

Opening a Bank Account
http://www.swissbanking.org/en/home/faq-kontoeroeffnung.htm

Travel by Train
http://www.sbb.ch/en/index.htm

Education in Switzerland
http://www.educa.ch/dyn/14.asp

Swiss National Library
http://www.nb.admin.ch/slb/index.html?lang = en

Swiss Government
www.admin.ch/

Chambers of Commerce and Industry
http://www.cci.ch/en/map.htm

Swiss Food
http://www.about.ch/culture/food/index.html

FURTHER READING

Websites

- http://www.admin.ch
  The mother of all sites as far as Swiss administrative, institutional, constitutional and historical questions are concerned. Goes on forever, but very well presented, and utterly reliable.

- http://www.justlanded.com/english/switzerland
  An English site for expats that gives endless, and usually sound, information on practical day-to-day questions on the country and how to handle things in it. Along with up-to-date information, the site gives you access to a forum on which you can post questions and get answers. This must be taken with a grain of salt obviously, but is nevertheless interesting.

- http://www.myswitzerland.com
  An American site with many pointers, often to touristic and cultural facilities, evaluations of restaurants and hotels and so on. Again with a forum which tells you how Hank and Doris from Milwaukee enjoyed Luzern.

- http://www.pro-helvetia.ch
  The site of the major centrally funded Swiss cultural foundation. As is the case with all official Swiss sites, it has an English-language version available.

- http://histoire-suisse.geschichte-schweiz.ch/
  Not available in English, but a brilliant history reference site, well indexed and footnoted.

- http://www.swissinfo.org
  Another big mamma site, with sound information on culture, lifestyle, food and drink, etc.

Books

- *The Xenophobe's Guide to the Swiss* (Paul Bilton), Orion Books, 1995. More for laughs than for facts, which are often wrong; nevertheless worth a quick read. Tends to work on stereotypes rather than facts.

- *Switzerland: A Guide to Recent Architecture* (Maya Huber, Thomas Hildebrand), 2001. Interesting, well-produced book on recent developments in Swiss architecture.

- *Recipes from a Master of French Cuisine* (F. Girardet). The greatest Swiss cook of the nouvelle cuisine school.

- *Walking Switzerland the Swiss Way* (Marcia & Phillip Lieberman), Mountaineer Books.

- *Grand Guide des Loisirs et des Vacances Suisse* (Kümmerly & Frey). A guide to trips on foot or bicycle; well-documented, with fine maps.

ABOUT THE AUTHOR

Swiss German, born in 1947, Max Oettli emigrated to New Zealand with his family when he was 10. After studying the humanities at the University of Auckland, he gained a considerable reputation in photography, which he has made his life's work. Returning to Switzerland in 1976, he was active as a photographer—specialising in architecture and town planning—and as a teacher in various institutions of higher learning. He lectured at the Geneva University of Technology for 27 years.

Married to the academic and writer, Simone Oettli van Delden, and with two grown sons, Max and his family lived on the outskirts of Geneva for 20 years. He was actively involved in politics on state and local levels, and was widely published both as a photographer and as a writer in his native country. His photographic work was seen mainly in calendars and architectural reviews, as well as a major book on Geneva's 20th-century architecture. His writing, mainly in French, has been on the interface of photography with various other cultural and political aspects of life.

Max left Switzerland for Dunedin, New Zealand in 2007, for a senior job at the Otago School of Art.

An enthusiastic if somewhat messy cook, Oettli's primary hobby is to enjoy life and pursue visual and cultural activities in different contexts.

INDEX

A

accommodation 5, 108–113
acronyms 224–226
alcohol 87

B

banking 42, 49, 50–3, 109, 113–4, 225
Basel 17, 24, 31, 32, 35, 44, 69, 90, 102, 108, 123, 144, 145, 155, 179–81, 184, 190, 197, 213, 216, 217, 221, 226
Bern 9, 10, 17, 32, 33, 34, 44, 47, 53, 63, 81, 104, 123, 139, 146, 161, 162, 179, 182, 184, 187, 189, 195, 197, 210, 214, 217, 226, 227

C

cantons 4, 29–34, 40, 45, 47–8, 90, 91, 100, 102, 104, 108, 110–20, 129, 152, 157, 162, 178, 183–185, 190, 195–6, 205, 226, 228
climate 18–19, 211
culture 178–182

D

dress code 168, 207
drinking 159–162
driving 62, 80, 91, 93, 127–133
drugs 85–86

E

eating out 162–165
education 17, 20, 37, 39, 49, 90, 119–122, 178

F

festivals 183–192
food 138–162
  cheese 61, 140, 144, 146, 148–157, 176, 186, 189, 190, 199
  chocolate 36, 56, 68–71, 74, 87, 139, 156, 176, 185
  fondue 152–6, 176
  sausages 93, 145
funerals 96–8, 175

G

gambling 86–87
Geneva 5, 6, 7, 13, 17, 19, 25, 31, 33, 36, 37, 39, 48, 50, 53, 54, 59, 73, 75, 82, 83, 86, 88, 89, 90, 97, 98, 102, 108, 109, 112, 123, 127, 144, 154, 157, 159, 160, 177, 178, 179, 182, 183, 184, 185, 188, 189, 191, 199, 205, 208, 213, 215, 216, 217, 218, 219, 222, 223, 224, 227
geography 13–17

H

health 20, 24, 39, 46, 49, 52, 82, 88, 101, 105, 115–19, 154, 178
history 25–43
holidays 183
homosexual relationships 97

I

Internet 7, 42, 60, 64, 78, 86, 111, 115, 129, 133, 136, 184, 192, 206

L

Lake Geneva 13, 25, 33, 86, 123, 154, 160, 185, 189, 223, 227
lakes 2, 5, 9, 13, 14, 19, 25, 29, 61, 177, 211, 227
lanaguage 193–201
Lausanne 7, 17, 43, 46, 61, 102, 106, 122, 123, 179, 182, 194, 195, 214, 223, 224, 227
Lucerne 19, 29, 31, 34, 44, 161, 179, 184, 187, 190, 194, 195, 227

M

Matterhorn 3, 159, 173
military service 76–81

P

population 7, 14, 17, 28, 31, 39, 45, 46, 48, 58–61, 70, 89, 104, 116, 178, 184, 211
prostitution 88

R

Red Cross 34, 39, 89, 136, 216, 227
refugees 38, 40, 72, 85, 90, 103, 213, 223
religion 89, 90, 211
  Catholicism 31, 32, 34, 89–90, 185, 191, 211, 227

Islam (Muslim) 89, 98, 119, 162, 211
Protestantism 32, 89, 90, 182, 211
residency permits 100–102

S

Saint Gallen 17, 28, 32, 35, 36, 228
shopping 45, 132, 133–137, 141–154
smoking 82–85
snow sports 174–178
Swiss army knife 10
Swiss-French 195, 197, 198, 220
Swiss-German 7, 9, 59, 61, 69, 80, 81, 89, 93, 94, 116, 123, 129, 146, 154, 156, 158, 185, 194–7, 199, 215, 219, 220, 226
Swiss-Italian 6, 7, 122, 131, 189, 215, 220

T

taxes 14, 46, 51, 90, 104–5, 109, 114–116, 119–20, 128, 130, 133, 203, 204, 223, 228
transport 121–133
    cars and driving 21, 22, 23, 62, 80, 87, 91, 93, 127–33, 163, 175, 177,
    cycling 10, 60, 109, 132, 135, 172
    railways 14, 20, 36, 46, 50, 121, 122, 200, 224, 225, 228

U

United Nations 17, 39, 227
utilities 109, 111

V

visual arts 213–214

W

wages 203–205
walking 19, 28, 94, 152, 167–174
watches 17, 68, 71–76, 133, 182, 213
weddings 96
work 203–208
World Health Organisation 39, 84, 215
World War II 37, 49, 78, 79, 223

Y

yodelling 150, 160

Z

Zürich 6, 10, 11, 17, 19, 24, 29, 31, 32, 34, 36, 37, 44, 47, 50, 51, 52, 59, 60, 68, 70, 108, 122, 123, 126, 127, 154, 158, 159, 160, 179, 182, 188, 197, 199, 213, 218, 220, 221, 222, 223, 228

Muslim 89, 98, 119, 162, 211

Titles in the CultureShock! series:

Argentina	France	Russia
Australia	Germany	San Francisco
Austria	Great Britain	Saudi Arabia
Bahrain	Hawaii	Scotland
Beijing	Hong Kong	Shanghai
Belgium	India	Singapore
Berlin	Ireland	South Africa
Bolivia	Italy	Spain
Borneo	Jakarta	Sri Lanka
Brazil	Japan	Sweden
Bulgaria	Korea	Switzerland
Cambodia	Laos	Syria
Canada	London	Taiwan
Chicago	Malaysia	Thailand
Chile	Mauritius	Tokyo
China	Morocco	Travel Safe
Costa Rica	Munich	Turkey
Cuba	Myanmar	United Arab
Czech Republic	Netherlands	Emirates
Denmark	New Zealand	USA
Ecuador	Paris	Vancouver
Egypt	Philippines	Venezuela
Finland	Portugal	

For more information about any of these titles, please contact any of our Marshall Cavendish offices around the world (listed on page ii) or visit our website at:

www.marshallcavendish.com/genref

Leabharlanna Poibli Chathair Bhaile Átha Cliath
Dublin City Public Libraries